OUR GIFTING ECLIPSE

Christian Essays

Marc Williams

BookLocker
Trenton, Georgia

Published by BookLocker.com, Inc., Trenton, Georgia, U.S.A.

Printed on acid-free paper.

BookLocker.com, Inc.
2023

CONTENTS

INTRODUCTION

We live in a strange time regarding the place of religion(s) and spirituality, both in our personal lives and in society generally. The 20th Century in many ways reduced the role of the Church to that of a spectator of all the changes and calamities brought about by culture, war and scientific advances. The clergy has tended to maintain the status quo in the face of these changes, remaining overly dogmatic and doctrinaire. Even as many congregants are leaving church and some sacrifice their spiritual lives in doing so, many members of the clergy remain steadfast in doing things the way they have always been done. The ongoing exodus from churches has been well-documented, but not well understood. For too many of us, church no longer benefits us, and so we have left, perhaps never to return. But what else to do instead? When I left church (again) nine years ago, I had no alternative in mind to bolster my spirituality. I just knew I couldn't go to church anymore, since all the clergy really had was the Bible, but they couldn't ever seem to adequately spell out its importance or relevance. Near the end, I had helped to hire our latest pastor, but could not see myself benefitting from her for the long-term. She was our best option, but not suitable for me. I realized after I left church that I never really had a good-enough pastor, and was not in the mood to spend time trying to find one, because I doubted there was one readily available. I was too tired of church to spend months or another year to go "church shopping," particularly as I live in a rural county, and was not going to drive but so far elsewhere. I say all of this because there is a lot of "church weariness" out there, and while most people still believe in God, outside of church how are we supposed to grow our own spirituality?

For a year before I left church, I had loosely begun reading books by various authors, but not in any coherent way. I had occasionally read religious books before then, but quite sporadically, having relied on church to give me spiritual enlightenment, as do most church-goers. Only later did I realize this had led to chronic spiritual malnourishment in ways I had not seriously considered. For example, we all have heard the phrase *Son of Man* spoken by Jesus in the Gospels, but I never knew where it came from when still going to church. It is, of course, from *Daniel 7:14*. I came to realize how badly unfocused is the usual presentation of Biblical material in church, aside from some depth in some Sunday School classes. Several of the pastors where I attended did not even teach Sunday School, which made such classes next to useless, and so I stopped going. What passes for "Christian education" in church can be a rather thread-bare experience.

After leaving church, I started reading more seriously. I soon read portions of John Calvin's tome, *Institutes of the Christian Religion* (1559), which in less than a year provoked me to write my own book. I discovered books by New Testament scholars which filled in some of the holes of my quite rudimentary "Christian education," broadening the 1st Century Jewish milieu, and prodded me toward some sharper spiritual understanding over the years. It has been from such scholarship that I have been able to start thinking on my own about what all this "Christian business" may be about, taking from their books enough to nudge me onto my own path. Scholars of particular value include E.P. Sanders, John Paul Meier, Raymond Brown, Craig Blomberg, Paul Anderson and especially Craig Keener, who actually has an anecdotal book about miracles. Without them and many others, I would not have gotten very far on my own. Reading the full Bible was also helpful, and finding the singular importance of John's Gospel was a revelation worthy of a lengthier essay.

Over the past five years, I have become interested in Judaism (and its "rebellious step-child," Messianic Judaism) from a Christian perspective, which is reflected in three of these essays. I have come to accept both the importance of Judaism as the "birthing cocoon" of Christianity as well as to recognize its limitations as being unlikely to truly comprehend the divine realm of God. I do not consider myself to be "anti-Jewish," but rather clearer-eyed about its practices and potential. It remains part of the overall problem of *religion for religion's sake*, which is contagiously pervasive. There simply has to be more than "reading about God in books."

*

I wrote my first book on Christian matters, *Once Every Day Becomes Easter* (2015), because I wanted to start sorting out both what I saw as wrong with the Church as well as to introduce psychology into the spiritual mix. I practiced psychotherapy for 37 years before retiring several years ago, and so it is natural for me to think in those terms about God and our spirituality. Other subjects I delved into included miracles, the Shroud of Turin and near-death experiences. This material helped me forge a synthesis of traditional and newer material toward a 21st Century Christianity that can sustain us better on the other six days of the week. New Testament academics also tend to spend too much time in their own cocoons, particularly in relation to all of the Shroud research over the last forty years. A few people are starting to connect the dots to flesh out all of this material into some kind of coherent whole, but "the elephant in the room" of God is always there — He waits (im)patiently for us to "figure Him out." This first book got me started on a clearer path, and while I largely stopped writing for three years afterward, I kept on reading and thinking.

Most of the 22 essays in this second book have been written in the last five years, being a sustained effort to harness and *clarify* all of this material into something that transcends mere religion(s) toward a spirituality that proclaims the divine realm of God to be our intended place of salvation, even beyond sin and redemption as portrayed in the Bible. There is the hallowed Trinity, the Puritans of the 17th Century, the New Testament Gospels and famous figures therein, and the most basic of Christian questions: who are God and Jesus Christ, and what is the actual relationship between Judaism and Christianity?

Underlying much of this material is the Freudian concept of *introjection,* discussed throughout many of these essays. Introjection is the foundation of all internalized and enacted religiosity, perhaps most clearly seen in the decades-long charitable work of Mother Teresa. It transcends religious beliefs, creeds and church services to form a muscular working style, whether individually or collectively, which infuses God into more of what we say and do, thus achieving the purpose of our faith — what people usually call "faith in action." This is a still-unique effort, but one which many people may well find appealing. Readers will notice there is some repetition of this material across these essays written months or years apart, reflecting the evolution of my spiritual journey. Comedians always tell their jokes more than once.

*

In the last essay, I talk at some length about all the "unknowables" about God, Jesus, the 1ˢᵗ Century Jewish milieu and the nature of Heaven. It is not hard to understand why people lose faith, since as I say, over and over, *God is invisible*, and we can not really introject His invisibility well enough to always sustain ourselves on a daily basis. The creeds are designed to deal with His invisibility by providing church-goers with the false certainty that repeating them could somehow "be enough," since even the Lord's Prayer — beautiful as it is — is not enough. The Bible is not enough, and praying can bring a sense of frustration and even desperation sometimes. God can be hard to hold onto, as His perpetual invisibility doesn't help. It can be a lot to ask of us, this faith stuff, and so spiritual malaise or atheism can be alluring for what it is not — no more questions or doubts, it all just stops. I went through such malaise and eventually came out on the other side, because such malaise eventually also proved to be too little to sustain me. *Something clicked* I say in this essay, and for the last ten years, I have been at least "spiritually okay," and usually more so.

I close this book with two of my (prose) poems, highlighting both God and Jesus as the spiritual focus of all we wish to both learn and at least aspire to perform in service to others. Only Christianity has a diviner figure-head who achieved a direct linkage to God, until the Jews find Him for themselves as their *Mashiach* as well.

Take what you can from these essays. They have been my great pleasure to write.

LEAVING CHURCH AND
BRINGING GOD WITH US

Several months ago, my wife and I left the Presbyterian church we had been attending for 12 years. While we seriously deliberated our decision for much of last year, once it was done, we felt relieved and had no second thoughts. We began our own little "home church" on Sunday mornings or evenings by listening to Internet sermons, discussing Christian topics of interest and having more frequent Communion. Our faith in God has not diminished, rather it needed richer nourishment and a keener sense of direction.

There are seemingly endless articles these days about the decline in church attendance and reasons why this is occurring, but little in-depth discussion from those who have actually done so. If Millennials were largely never given much exposure to Christianity or church, then we baby boomers have often lost our spiritual way during our adult years by going to church mainly because we are supposed to. Church services too often feel like passive spectator hours of "the monotony of performances" by others, and it is too common to leave a church service feeling spiritually entertained, but not divinely inspired.

Frankly, the quality of the clergy can be naggingly problematic, not because of their incompetence, but rather from too seldom providing any overarching clarity to Biblical or other Christian material. Pastors feel threatened by popular culture, by television and increasingly by science, clinging to the Bible as their only province of knowledge and teaching. They tend to erect a fortress or cocoon, within which are spun weekly webs of Scriptural puzzles of Biblical symbolism — nice knowledge but hardly the full embodiment of Jesus working in the world.

Changes in the church often move at a glacial pace because no one person speaks for the clergy as a whole. Even Pope Francis will likely have varying degrees of influence on particularly the Protestant clergy, despite his ecumenical message of concern for the poor and afflicted.

7

It is wearying to "wait for what never comes," for any pastor's clarity of vision and action to thrust us forward with an emboldened sense of Christian purpose for Mondays and beyond. I will let others complain about what else goes on in church that is either hypocritical or merely deflating, although I am tired of hearing "the clergy are broken people, too."

I had previously left church as a teenager, not returning for 20 years, and so have always known the difference between God and church. Most of what interests me about the Christian faith I have learned on my own. What has roused me the most intensely has, ironically, come from television: the lengthy 1977 NBC biographical film, *Jesus of Nazareth,* and *The Real Face of Jesus,* a 2010 History Channel documentary about the scientific work done on the Shroud of Turin. I first learned about the Shroud nearly thirty years ago, and felt voltage from its mystery which has never left me, even when scientists declared it was a fake from carbon dating in 1988, which in recent years has been proven to be unreliable.

The Shroud and the unexplained near-death experiences of too many to ignore are frothing our desire to again ask the big questions: What does God do in the world? How does He deal with our prayers? If He indeed created the universe and our Earth through a long evolutionary process while accepting our constant sinfulness and distrust of Him, how does God remain patient with our worldly philandering? We know our own psychology throws up nests of barbed wire to keep God at bay, not being sure we want an all-knowing Father meddling in our embarrassing personal business but so much, despite our well-meaning prayers.

What we need beyond praise services with taffy songs, bland sermons and the vagaries of "spiritual relevance" is to answer basic Christian questions with a clarity greater than pat Scripture passages or tautological theology. Neither John Calvin, Dietrich Bonhoeffer nor C.S. Lewis (all of whom I have read recently) quite take us to the burning candle: God's Holy Mystery. We can not fashion Christian faith on our own, as though by baking a loaf of bread or endlessly praising God merely at loud choral volume, since such faith has to come from God first. To be simple, *we need His proof.* Anyone who doubts Jesus was crucified and resurrected only needs to discover the Shroud research from the past 35 years. Seeing the moment when Jesus stops suffering and ascends into Heaven, contrasting His peaceful face from His tortured body is, for me, where our faith begins. Not faith without sight, as even Jesus himself said, but rather seeing Him then and there, in that bloody and wondrous circumstance, *is* believing.

The Holy Mystery is the unwavering presence of what God radiantly offers to us, whether we go to church or stay home, He telling us: I *am with you through all that goes on, I feed you in all manners of sustenance, so how can I be ignored?* Atheists can not yet find this Mystery, but don't humor them by saying it doesn't exist. Just tell them to go watch an aurora borealis in a field of lilies, where *God's Heavenly light dances in the darkness.*

Summer 2014

THOUGHTS ABOUT CHRISTIANITY

question: "Have you ever experienced divine intervention"?

- 40% (free will) ------ 40% (Bible) ----- 20% (Shroud of Turin / near-death events)

---

psychology portion: we are the "living hosts" of God and Jesus on earth, His faith is placed in us to do His work in the world — by giving us **free will**, we can accept or reject God and Jesus, partially or fully, to live our lives as we must. God thought long and hard before placing us at the end of the evolutionary chain, because free will could cause us to cleave ourselves from Him (Adam and Eve) for our own purposes. The 20th Century began the decline of religious faith in God because of what we have come to be able to do for ourselves. Technology tends to warp or kill our faith in God. Doctors can heal people without God. We become increasingly selfish and "power-full" from what we can accomplish on our own, such that God does not feel so necessary. He allows us to do what we want, without obvious consequences from Him (re: Old Testament). Thus, God gets ignored or forgotten too often. God's *"complacency": He allows so much to simply happen — why bad things happen to us.*

- *the Father problem:* children become ambivalent over the power of their fathers to continually influence them (particularly during adolescence), and will rebel to assert some independence. With our *unseen* God, the likelihood of "rebellion" (disinterest) is greater because He no longer reaches down to grab us by the collar to correct us. God gave up being a disciplinarian by the end of the Old Testament, because it did not work. Instead, He decided to use Jesus to better influence us in the flesh. We are reluctant to readily accept the necessity

11

of a "second (unseen) Father," particularly in our 20s and 30s. Maturationally, *God becomes memorable.*

- *the Bible:* 66 books, 750,000-plus words, no pictures — allegorical / mythological stories in the Old Testament (none of which are independently corroborated) about Jews who struggle to maintain faith in God over hundreds (and nearly thousands) of years of adversity. The New Testament is much more compressed in time (3 years, plus an unclear later post-Jesus period for Acts and Paul). The Bible is wonderfully chocked with stories and descriptions, with threadbare narratives that are believable to the extent of their uniqueness. The Bible moves from the stories to the life of Jesus in an increasingly realistic manner until we reach the Crucifixion and Resurrection. The Bible allows us to be introduced at great length to the will and purpose of God for us as a great start to our faith.

- *How healthy are we* to accept God's purpose for ourselves (psychologically)? If we are not healthy enough, all the Bible-reading we can do will not matter so much, it will not enable us able to serve others because of our own narcissism.

- *near-death experiences and the Shroud of Turin* (20%) as the clearest evidence of God's influence, since we could never have created the world (universe) ourselves. How God "dips" into our lives to unilaterally surprise us sometimes. For me, this became the "proof" of God's existence and purpose.

2014

NUDGING THE DOCTRINE OF THE TRINITY TO GREATER CLARITY

The Trinity, as a conceptual effort to better understand Jesus' own use of "Father, Son and Holy Spirit" in Matthew 28:19 regarding baptism (its only appearance in the Gospels), has a very long history, dating back to at least the early Christian thinker Tertullian in ca. 200 C.E., when he coined the term *trinitas.* Although I do not agree with its basic premise of "three independent yet co-existing Persons," I have come to understand its desire to make better sense of who God and Jesus are in the territory of the human-divine realm.

A main objection to the Trinity is that the term itself does not appear in the New Testament, yet the Matthew verse seems sufficient to allow it to serve as the foundation, since it is Jesus Himself who introduces this idea quasi-conceptually. He wants us to more seriously consider the divine realm, with which the Jews of his time were at best rudimentarily familiar in their own writings, as for them, it was still more an idea than an experience. Jesus shows us *the divine realm in person as His experience* through His miracles, in particular. I have recently come to understand that we can not simply reject the Trinity because it "came later" after Jesus — no, I do think He introduces it conceptually, yet does not elaborate upon it much at all. He does want us to consider it, though. Jesus is primarily interested in our spiritual transformation, after all.

I will begin with the Holy Spirit, because its "independence" likely does not exist. I would say that the Holy Spirit is an expression of God's will, rather than an independent force or entity, since no one has ever conceptualized the Holy Spirit's "independence," and indeed, it hardly gets discussed at all. In John's Gospel, Jesus mentions "the Advocate" to the disciples after His resurrection, again without elaboration. This reduces the Trinity to its proper focus, that of the nature of the human-divine realm.

Several years ago, I read a book entitled *No One Sees God*, the sentiment of which serves as the host for our consideration of the Trinity. We can not see the nature of the human-divine realm unless we (literally) witness Jesus (which hardly anyone does these days) or a miracle performed by God. The basis for the Trinity is the super-naturally miraculous, it functions outside our own influence and is not explicable by scientific notions or measurements. God provides us with spiritual sustenance in ways we humans can not do by ourselves. Jesus Himself is the only figure who has ever embodied the human-divine realm, hence the Trinity tries to explain His nature as a summation of His mission on Earth, trying to answer this nagging question of *who is Jesus?*

To be clear: Jesus was and is not God Himself. His divinity came in the last years of His life during His mission to His fellow Jews and eventually the Gentiles. It is a steady transfusion of Spirit likely over his entire lifetime, culminating in the wisdom and miracles of His mission. How do I know this? Gods do not get flogged and crucified, gods do not bleed "blood and water," gods do not get resurrected because gods never die, and gods are persuasive in ways Jesus was not: to His disciples and other followers, the Pharisees and the Romans. While Jesus does singularly straddle the human-divine realm, His divinity is one-directional from God, and He admits this repeatedly in John's Gospel. This is where the Trinity breaks down conceptually, because it loses track of these facts. Nonetheless, I still find it useful, and admire those who have perused it through all the many centuries, since it is an effort to make sense of what we can never humanly see.

*

So, an alternative. By our time, after post-Lutheran religious wars as well as science, medicine and the endless theological speculations of very learned men, any Christian doctrines must now be strained through that nagging, very mystical question: *what really happened in the Tomb*? I would say that Jesus was *always necessarily special* in the Biblical description, but what about His "apprenticeship" (ages 12-30), before which there is no evidence of either ministry or miracles, nor any proof of divinity? It does me no good to think that He had already been eternal since the creation of the universe, but had never shown Himself until just before Herod the Great died, after the Maccabean revolt had energized the Israelites, but were now again threatened by Herod Antipas? Jesus is born of a human mother (whether virginal or not — either way is fine with me), retains "ordinary" human form throughout His life, and evolves ("wisdom and stature") until God tells Jesus at His baptism it is now His time to (try and) save the world. It takes Him a long time to even reveal to His disciples that He is the Son of God. I don't think they would have accepted the Trinity idea, struggling as they were, since Jesus was always way beyond them, anyway. His ministry unfolds until and through Holy Week.

The disciples eventually reject Jesus precisely because they can not "straddle the gap" between the human and divine which He presents them, so it is really no surprise that He is rejected by the Sanhedrin. Judas Iscariot to me is not "the worst person ever born," but rather represents our collective doubt about human claims of divinity. Jesus then dies the worst (fully human) death imaginable (the first time I read a detailed medical description of crucifixion, I fainted for the only time in my life), and everything implodes. Why is it called Good Friday? Jesus has to die, still only human, for the divinely miraculous to happen. I have never been happy with the idea that He "triumphed over death" — He didn't, rather He died terrorably, at the nadiring point to make us accept the viability of Easter on Sunday. Jesus becomes divine after being dead in the tomb by "an act of God."

So what is that "act of God?" Physicists doing Shroud research speak of what they call an "event horizon," in which gravity is momentarily suspended to allow Jesus to rise off the rock, with the tautened Shroud completely around Him, and, in a millisecond, His bodily image is projected onto the linen, front and back sides (without distortions) with the radiation of a small sun. He ascends (after grilling fish on the beach) to remain in Heaven with God, perhaps forever. His post-Resurrection appearances to either Mary or at Emmaus seem to reflect his varying "state of matter." Ask a physicist.

In a solar system analogy, God is the sun, Jesus is Mercury, and the rest of us are other planets, depending on our faith (I used to be out beyond Saturn, in my younger years). Jesus always hovers in the tightest orbit around God, which shrinks and shrinks throughout His life, and collapses altogether at the moment of His Resurrection. He then is swallowed into the sun, perhaps forever. For me, there is no "fully human, fully divine" Jesus, there is only His "evolving toward the divine" until it actually happens, under the auspices of God. As a man, Jesus can not affect the weather, bring forth birth or change the laws of chemistry or gravity by Himself. He did not create them, God did. Jesus did not claim to be God, even at the point of death. He was God's begotten Son, and there is a very real difference. He was an electro-magnet, not of His own creation, but of His very necessary embodiment. I think this is what "the beloved disciple" understood in the Tomb (and in the Upper Room) in the greatest piece of Scripture: *John 20: 1-9.* Jesus' evolution thus provides an example for our own spiritual journeys, since none of us will ever be divine, at least in this earthly life.

Since Jesus has the numeral "3" on His forehead on the Shroud, I could certainly be wrong about all of this. Is this about "I spent three days in the tomb, and rose?" John's Gospel portrays God's "spiritual transfusion" into Jesus over three Passovers, eventually resulting in His clear-cut, post-resurrection divinity to His apostles, Paul and others. Jesus straddles the chasm between the human and divine, as no one else does. I think Arius at the Council of Niacea in 325 C.E. was more right than not, though he was shouted down. Since then, theologians have often gotten too bogged down in the intricacies of the Trinity, forgetting that we are actually trying to answer Jesus' own question to us: *do you want to be more spiritualized human beings, or not?*

2016; extensively revised: 2020

JOHN THE BAPTIST

What is the place of John the Baptist in the trajectory between the Old and New Testaments? What does his work say about God's frustration with us after His long attempts, through both stories and prophecies, to persuade us to follow Him in the OT essentially fail? The OT tries but fails to go deep enough through both resistance to God generally and through bouts of idol worship against Him in our need for "transitional representations" of who we can not see for ourselves. This is no small problem, of course, which still plagues us today. Jesus later faced this even from His disciples, who saw everything. There are the differences between conjuring, seeing and understanding, and all Jews and Christians suffer from "the useless necessity of imagination" with God.

The ca. 150-year gap between the end of the OT and John the Baptist gave God plenty of time to come up with a new idea: bodily (and increasingly less slight) approximations of Himself on earth, first through John and then Jesus. He wanted to get past the "we can't see You" problem, since this dogged Adam and Eve in the Garden from the beginning. Free will, for and against God, comes from "You are too invisible" beyond the physical world. I read a book several years ago with the obvious title of *No One Sees God*, but its meaning reverberates through every religion, and tends to supplant mystery with doctrine. You would know better than me if the OT prophets ever ventured out amongst the people in the manner of John, or "merely wrote" their concerns.

Regarding John, it would be quite useful to know the length of his own efforts prior to Jesus' baptism, simply as a starting point for how he is uniquely different from the OT prophets. The trio of "complaining" (or, more Biblically, exhortative) prophets (being Isaiah, Jeremiah and Ezekiel) are both summarized in John beyond mere writing, but also in the flesh as perhaps the first example of "word becomes flesh." Instead of those who can not read Scripture being left behind, John leaves his (apparent) father, Zechariah, behind to go into the wilderness to "feed the people" directly. Scholar John Paul Meier states that the crowds found John to be fascinating, perhaps because of the style (locusts and honey) as well as his introduction of baptism (an action, not only reading) to the Jews. He is thus a "walking advertisement" for what God now is asking for from His people: *do not simply read about Me, I send you this man to give you guidance.* Meier thinks that John also offered them advice about how to pray and how to deal with the "concrete morality" concerns of daily life.

Meier doubts the Mary—Elizabeth dual-pregnancy story is historical, and thinks it was fabricated by the early Christian church later on to solidify the relationship between John and Jesus. He is inclined to think that Jesus spent perhaps several months with John's group, having traveled to Galilee from Nazareth to find out about him and, ultimately, to be baptized. Jesus also came to understand John's "only human" limitations (no miracles), but saw him as a foundation for what He wanted to do Himself. The old question is: how much did Jesus know of His mission prior to being baptized? Clearly, John gives Jesus permission to challenge the commonplace Jewish sentiments of their time, and not remain hamstrung by doctrines, the Law and social customs. John chastises his fellow Jews as a preface to what Jesus will later do with the Pharisees, in particular, some of whom, rather ambivalently, come to John to be baptized (Matthew 3:7). Whether John sees himself as a new prophet, such as Elijah, is unclear, yet seems to think that, through this new-fangled baptism, he is "on to something" from God. In doing psychotherapy, there is always the question of patients' capacity for *transcendent function*, meaning to outgrow the negative impact of their histories toward any better psychological status. In a slight sense, John provides the Israelites a new version of the OT prophets within which to see if such transcendence becomes more possible, both in-person and through baptism.

For me, John represents God's changing His mind about how to affect people, which has ramifications for the clergy. If the OT is primarily exhortative, John represents the embodiment of this style in a visible person, but he offers something more: that baptism is a ritual which begins to shrink the Jews' resistance through doing rather than merely reading and thinking — it is a step beyond exhortation to buy into a physicalized symbolism that says: why else would you do this, submerge your psyche (soul?) to be cleansed, if not for God? Baptists today tend to insist on full immersion for this reason: the resistance gets diminished (at least temporarily) as an introduction to "sighting the divine." For each clergy-person, John and Jesus tell you, beyond OT exhortation, to draw your flocks to you, do not be afraid to be Spiritually magnetic, but be sure you have something to offer them once they do come, because, if not, they will turn away. The Catholic clergy has remained overly exhortative, and it has cost them so much, since we have all met "lapsed Catholics" who drifted away from such exhortations. Meier, as have other recent scholars, digs deeper to make better sense of who John and Jesus were, and is not content to merely recycle Christian traditions, which is what interests me.

Christians are not the Israelites awaiting their Messiah, since we already have One. Borrow from John and Jesus what you can for us, but exhortation, in our age of television's constant advertising, will no longer work. It never really did.

*

In my sense of the old concept of *metanoia*, repentance actually comes *after* the insightful need to accept Jesus and God, not before. Otherwise, it is: why are we repenting, and it may well not stick. Idol worship functioned as our human need for physicalized representations of God to see and touch (see Ezekiel 14:6, which has this backwards). In psychology, this is referred to as "transitional objects," like stuffed animals for young children. Idol worship was necessary for the Israelites to adapt to monotheism until *"someone* better" (John and

Jesus) came along. This is why Protestants wear crosses or Catholics use rosary beads. We can not imagine God well enough to suit us, doctrines or not. Even Jesus confused the disciples too much until after the resurrection, and only then they willingly died for Him.

God says *use My people and not only your ideas about Me, since too much of what you think about Me is too far off the mark.* Ask anyone who has visited Heaven and come back to tell us about it. It is almost entirely unimaginable. So is God.

2016

OUR UNRAVELING PURITY

I am finishing up reading a book about the Puritans, which focuses on their sense of persecution in England and coming to what will become Massachusetts in the 1620s to establish a sense of freedom here to develop a Bible-based society. The Puritans thought of themselves as "the new Israelites," and saw "the New World" as a living doctrinal church society and a kind of Christian utopia in the harsh New England countryside as their "promised land." Many died either on the voyages over here or in the early years from the winters and lack of growable food, yet their determination was great. During their early years, the Puritans tried to establish what they called "the well-ordered family" as the basis for a small Christian society, which, of course, demanded regular church involvement. Those who wanted to join a congregation had to pass what amounted to a kind of oral examination from either the pastor or the congregation collectively. A kind of Baptist testimony was offered as to one's sense of spiritual conversion. Sermons are described as lengthy and sometimes soporific.

There were many laws enacted to encourage righteous behavior in public. Punishments for infractions could be severe. There were death penalties for the following: adultery, for teenagers who knowingly cursed or disrespected their parents, for being a witch, and for homosexual behavior. Reasoning about such laws came directly from Old Testament scripture, literally chapter and verse. The Puritans were also quite superstitious and worried about the Devil's activities, which would later contribute to the Salem Witch Trials of 1692-93.

The Puritans derived their sense of Christian faith directly from John Calvin, whose *Institutes of the Christian Religion* was published in 1559, and apparently was translated from Latin into English quickly enough to become part of the Anglican theology with which the Puritans struggled before coming over here. Having read a fair portion of *Institutes* myself, it does have a peculiar attractiveness in its attempt to whittle down the Jewish preoccupation with (613) laws as well as the Catholic preoccupation with liturgical services and décor to actually make Christianity understandable to "the masses" with simpler doctrinal material. Although I criticized Calvin in my own book, I do see that he is trying to move our faith from an expansive legal and religious framework toward something we can better "hold in our hands." The problem is that, in practice with the Puritans, it still led to actual laws not unlike those of the Israelites, which people could (and did) then disobey.

Given that some 1,600 years go by between the death of Jesus and the Puritans, we could ask: is the Church too humanly-centered in its understanding of who God is and what He is trying to do with us? Whether it is the Israelites, the Catholics or the Puritans, they all have one problematic thing in common: *let us teach you how to be while ignoring the particular person that you are.* If there is a singular difference between the Church and psychotherapy, it is that I can not ignore who the patient is in favor of "some idea" I have to give them about themselves. I do not expect the clergy to be therapists, but what you are now faced with are people who will not be psychologically ignored in favor of any doctrinal prescriptions.

Like everything else, Christian faith exists in the context of one's psychology — they are twined together like any other preferences or prejudices we have. It would be easy to devise sermons in this context which would draw in the congregation through psychological generalities of experiences, doubts and inspirations. Freud called this *introjection*, which means that we absorb influences from others (such as our parents) which go deep enough to affect our behavior, even when they are absent. Introjections can be positive or negative, of course. When Jesus uses the analogy of blindness and sight ("those who believe without seeing"), He is taking about our introjecting Him as a spiritual influence, which is sometimes done in a personal context.

The Puritans eventually imploded within 70 years because they could not address their people's need for more than Church teachings and laws, which eventually bred rebellion and / or indifference. Ironically, they became too human in their conception of God, which has gotten the Jews, Catholics and Protestants in too much trouble. One of the themes in my own book was *God was never human.*

The Catholic contemplatives around this same time tried a different route, but having read Saint John of the Cross' *Dark Night of the Soul* (1619) myself, this becomes a bit muddy and speculative for me as to what is ours and what is God's, though I am admittedly no mystic.

*

I have been following the just-completed Methodist General Conference, which lamely ended with no real attempt to bridge the ca. 865 delegates' divisions on "the gay issue," rather they decided to try to settle such an issue by a study committee, which will never work. The problem that all the various Catholic and Protestant faiths have had on this issue comes from asking the wrong questions. The clergy never asks: *Why are there homosexuals, and what purpose do they have in God's vision for us? If they can not be inherently procreative, what other purpose might He have for them?* Rather, it is as it has always been: *suppress what you do not understand.* With gay Methodist pastors now "coming out" and risking their careers, this will continue in the face of no organized response from their church. Psychology triumphs over doctrine, for better and worse.

Any prejudice stems from our narcissism, from *who we are not.* The historical bias against homosexuals runs deeper than all others because of our general lack of genital attraction to others of the same sex. This runs deeper than skin color, nationality, language or other attributes — it is rooted in our very biology. Since God allows for many things (diseases, Natural disasters, crime and the death of His Beloved Son), homosexuality would seem to be another such example. Why do bad things happen to good people? Because God is not Calvin's micromanager, He set the conditions for our world to work, He intervenes when necessary, and yes, allows things to happen. There is free will and there is God. There are no false dichotomies with God, He simply does what He wants and does not ask for either our permission or "blessing." It is we who must someday catch up with Him.

May 2016

ONCE EVERY DAY BECOMES THE LAST
(a fictional meditation)

As a physician for many years, I have at times been faced with patients suffering from terminals diseases who will soon die. While we are taught to help such patients and their families during these very difficult times, each situation is unique and so we have to be prepared yet flexible.

Like most everyone else, we physicians often don't think about the end of our own lives unless we are also faced with such a situation. Almost everyone thinks they are somehow immune from death until it becomes clear otherwise. We are very talented bodily repairers who pride ourselves on our special abilities to fix what makes others feel so helpless. When patients die, we often ask ourselves whether we might have failed in some way, though generally the answer is *no*. Too often, people just die.

To wake up to find out this would be the last day of my life would be frighteningly horrible, especially if I was reasonably healthy and cognizant beforehand. For this exercise, we will say that I have a worsening disease that becomes terminal, rather than an unexpected accident that kills me. My disease worsens, and my own physician tells me that it is terminal, and one morning I wake up to find out it is today that I will die. It dawns on me that today is my last one. The sun rises as always, and yet I will die, today. This is all I can grasp so early, and I know I will end up wasting too much time today, my last one, trying to grasp its meaning. Life is always about grasping its meanings.

We will say that it is then that I remember to fulfill a request to write about what my life has been like, what it has meant to me, and how others might better live your lives. It is perhaps feeble advice given in the midst of a personal shatter-time. My head spins every moment because I will be dead by midnight. Time stops. I will stay up, if I can, until midnight because time stops. It is all today, present time. Wisdom never felt so sickly.

*

In the span of really no time, I must summon some ability to reflect upon my life, from its beginnings in boyhood, through marriage, children and medical practice to try to suddenly answer that old question: *What has been the purpose of my life?* On any other day, this would be easily put off and promised for some future time to more seriously consider. But today, it is now or death. I will do this as quickly as I can, since I have much else to do. *You shall die today*, someone else keeps saying, the worst mantra.

What I figured out in my childhood was that I was smart, that I had a future with which to contribute to public health, and so studied hard to get that going. I had the beginnings of a personal purpose as a teenager, studied hard in high school, and thought about what being a doctor would entail. I would see sick people and corpses, I would see fright and hear screaming, I would try to console patients and give others the best news. Later on, I wanted to marry another doctor who understood the dreams I had, who was not afraid of sickness, death and seeing the insides of people. Medical people have to have a stomach most others can not, well, stomach. I knew I would be an important person who truly helped people, sometimes saving their lives. Performing surgery itself is a strangely singular talent to focus to help someone I barely know. Sometimes I will be remembered forever by patients whose faces and names are often only briefly familiar. All I knew was that I wanted to do this work, that sometimes it would be hard, but I knew it was important and I could truly make a difference in peoples' lives, unmistakably so.

Through all the years of medical training and subsequent practice, everything and nothing has changed. The hours are long, the demands are heavy, I probably neglect my own family at times, but they try to understand. The work is its own reward, it is still what I must do for a livelihood, to stop being a doctor would have been to kill my soul. What else could I purposefully do? To that degree, I have had a good life, until today. Today is a bad day, the worst day, because all of that stops, forever. If I go to Heaven at midnight, I will not be a doctor there, since God does not need this from me anymore. I will be like everyone else there. Doctors are special you know, that's why we are called "M.D.," for "Me, Doctor." But God creates the bodies that I repair, I could never do that, so I have to become more humble before midnight. I still have a little time.

*

I am being asked to give you some life lessons, particularly from the perspective of a physician who has loved my work. I could talk about being a husband and father, about trying to balance work and home life (better) or what it is like to live in America for foreigners to try to understand our life here. But I will offer what I can as a physician, because it is a very unique job, and affects everything I can tell you.

Do your best to fashion a personal purpose in your life as soon as possible. Or really the capacity to have such a purpose, since its form and texture may well change with time and age. Don't be afraid to be serious and ambitious about what is achievable, within reason, as what your lives must be about. Having fun by itself is not enough, nor even being in love. Plenty of people are in love, but still have no larger purpose. It is not an either / or. Love and purpose are both important and necessary, they are what keep us going, and what now allows me it say anything useful to you at all.

Don't waste time. I don't mean seconds or minutes, but days, weeks, months and years of time. If I can die peaceably on this my last day, it is through knowing that I have not unnecessarily wasted time in my life. To not be self-destructive is so important. Those who become suicidal have lost their purpose, and become hopeless about getting it back, so keep your purpose and use of time in mind all the time.

Befriend and love those who have something to offer you, and reject those who sap your energy. This sounds selfish, and it is, but you will not help such people by befriending them in their dispiriting manner. Befriend those who offer you themselves in a positive way, particularly if you can gain something new from them. Friendships are reciprocal in the best cases, not one-sided. To give and to receive.

Finally, know that God made you to serve Him on this earth in your best capacity, so stop wasting His time.

July 2017

WHO IS GOD?

Long before any religion formed and named itself, whether pagan or monotheistic, there was our Natural world. Our earliest sense of God's divinity came once men and women recognized that we were both different than other creatures yet part of the larger Natural whole, easily witnessed both on the ground as well as in the seas and sky. We could walk and talk, think for ourselves and yet, each evening, accepted our dependence on what God provided us in terms of food and makeable shelter. What I have called the chasm between the human and the divine is always most evident where we have to fend for ourselves in unfamiliar, rugged or watery places, far from our modern suburban comforts. This formed perhaps the purest sense of our Godly worship, how we necessarily had to introject (purpose-fully absorb) Him because there was no ability to fashion for ourselves anything separate from what He gifted us for daily living. Primitive men introjected images of horses and cattle (as seen in the Paleolithic caves in France and Spain) as what God was for them. Such art-work was neither pagan nor theological — rather these images represented for the primitives the unbendable connection with He who provided sustenance in food and weather, which they themselves could not. There was great curiosity about the world from this acceptance of their Natural dependency. There were, however, as yet no named God or gods, no divine beings from "somewhere else in the sky," no theological doctrines or rituals performed to "serve" Him. All of that would come much later over thousands of years. First, we had to find God as a divine being.

*

Until the Jews, there was no single God who reigned in Heaven to offer His people hope and promise for our human future. Their concept of a monotheistic God, given to Abraham and later channeled into the *Shema*, represented a radical re-ordering of divine purpose from the

Egyptians and later the Greeks, whose gods were estranged from our human doings and "mostly played around in the sky, causing mischief." Praying to a single God, instead of humanly ignoring a panoply of gods, up-ended our sense of what was Godly possible: that now He could be prayed to and worshipped as the divine influence upon whom we could remain beholden. Whether or not the Abraham story is historically true, Jesus later confirmed its purpose: to link us to a singular God, who would bore into our lives on occasions of His choosing to "set us right" in His image. This Jewish contribution, for me, makes every poly-theistic religion use-less as works of theological conjecture and thus "unprovable."

Judaism, because of its excessive use of religious laws and doctrinal decisions, itself largely withered after Jesus' resurrection, because He had usurped what could be studied and obediently performed with a living person who showed us what God wanted us to do. Jesus is not merely "replacement theology," He transcended Jewish oral and written laws with "the mouth of God" in His flesh — not only words, but miracles and bodily resurrection through and beyond His death on the Cross. Judaism sometimes tried to shed its skin as a "mere religion," but never caught up with where God told it to go as encouraged by the Old Testament prophets, particularly regarding idolatry. Its original 613 laws became their idolatry, but with an admittedly better intended purpose. Judaism became another theological cocoon, with more to come otherwise. Everything we think about God is likely at least half-wrong, if His signature is nowhere to be found.

Catholicism replaced these 613 Jewish laws with sometimes strange, questionably tenable notions about how God works and how we are to serve Him. There is the Pope, there is celibacy, there is purgatory and there is transubstantiation, among others. Like Judaism (its parental influence, really), Catholicism is complex and demanding, in some ways more abstract and yet also too absolute. It singularly offers a human intermediary (the Pope) who, lacking any verifiable sense of divinity, espouses a historically repressive lifestyle and too few genuine answers to life's perplexing questions. While Judaism shackles its followers with too many things to do on a daily basis (such as during Passover), Catholicism spins itself around certain ideas which do not lend any greater certainty to the value of God beyond repeating such ideas in seemingly endless combinations of "this and that." On the few occasions that I have attended Mass, I experience both the emphasis on "Catholic pageantry" and often the sense of my life draining out of me, knowing this basic ritual has been performed millions of times around the world for sinners like you and me. Celibacy for priests and nuns is based upon the especially wrong-full notion that sexual orgasm is to be "conquered" through perpetual abstinence, as though this actually makes any serious difference in our righteous service to others. God gave us a penis and clitoris not to be ignored, but to be enjoyed, with whom and when it makes sense to do so. Transubstantiation, in its most literal translation, becomes a hallucinatory act of conjuring Jesus' body and blood into what we can hold and taste across nearly 2,000 years of His physical absence. Communion is meant to remember Him, not to push the Spiritual envelope into quasi-psychotic absurdity. Purgatory, a uniquely Catholic idea, makes no sense to me at all.

Having been raised as a Presbyterian and attending three of its churches before and around lengthy absences, it is a sense of paler Protestant faith drawn from church that I know best. There are no religious laws, fewer overarching ideas and only two sacraments: baptism and Communion, instead of Catholicism's seven rituals. While Martin Luther and John Calvin arguably made "improvements" in the liturgical style of the Catholic Mass, their own dogmatic biases overlaid much constriction upon the worshipping lives of the Protestants, and almost certainly contributed to the Puritans' eventual implosion after the Salem witch trials. Charges of "white bread Protestantism" rang truer through the mid-20th Century, and the long, painful and now accelerating exodus from their churches has occurred over the past fifty years. Whereas the Jewish and Catholic faiths overloaded their faithfull with too much "regulation," the Protestants have been rightly accused of blandness, "relativism," and no coherent message or purpose beyond "come to church every Sunday." It is this "monotony of performances" that I finally had to abandon some four years ago — irritated every time I went because nothing much ever happens. It has become church with no real purpose. I came to understand why Jesus trusted the wayward Peter more than merely building a church.

*

As I described in my book, *Once Every Day Becomes Easter* (2015), the long and longest efforts to fill the chasm between the human and the divine with theological speculations, religious laws and strict-spun practices has not resolved the most basic questions we still face: who is God, and how does He actually work in the world and our lives; can we affect Him in any way, whether through prayer or our actions in aiding others; and what is this place called Heaven? Admittedly, all the speculation felt necessary because there is little clear way to know anything about God except what He actually does, so I will start with that: perhaps it is better to work backwards from the more obvious acts of God toward any reasons to explain Him. If religion were at least a little more like science — facts before theories — this might prove more useful, even if such "science" only goes so far. What I am really tired of is the clergy hanging onto such theologies with no clear sense that they ever really occur. Maybe personal testimonials can play a role in such "science," for example, Jews who accept Jesus after reading the New Testament, and being surprised to find out that He and the disciples were Jewish. *Really.*

So, I come back to the Natural world. By now, we can assume that God created the universe in general and our Earth in particular. Scientists tell us the chances of biological life being created at random are miniscule. There is a Natural order which remains recurringly sensible and sustains us over days and centuries. In his book, *Finding Darwin's God* (1999), Catholic biologist Kenneth Miller states: "the study of

Nature is akin to the worship of God," and so it more profitable to start with what He made to find the origins of His divinity, long before Judaism, the Bible and all the theological rancor, some of which I have recently learned resulted in Christians killing Jews in the Middle Ages. God, of course, would have had no interest in religious wars fought in His name, since He never told us to explain Him, only to obey through serving others. Ask an atheist how gravity was created, and they will merely look at you, dumb-founded.

If we accept a God-made universe and the basic tenets of the evolution of life over millions of years (finally agreeing that the Genesis story of Adam and Eve was the Israelites' attempt to explain our human origins, in ca. 1700-1200 B.C., and so for them such a story was mythically necessary — no more and no less), I come back to why He wanted to create we human beings at all — yes, in His own image, but why? He could have stopped and stuck with the other mammals, and suffered so much less soul-ache from our stupidity and trying to render Him modernly irrelevant. Why did God want to "drink the gamble" that we could become truly devoted to Him as a larger populace without idolatry and other distractions, that all religions could be boiled down to a basic acceptance of who He is and why He matters to us? He always knew that we would daily fail Him in countless ways, so why bother at all? It is circular: God had to create us to see if we could worship and serve Him to render plain the possibility that He would truly matter on a human level. The problem is that He does and (for us) He does not matter, because we are solipsistically human, and, too often in our machinal world, don't need Him to survive and even thrive. He gave us our human lives to thrive in Him.

Last night, I went to an Ash Wednesday service at our local Catholic church. It was well attended by a mixture of older white and Hispanic parishioners, with a seasoned priest who was, shall we say, less than humble. The service last 25 minutes, and presented familiar material and an amusing but disjointed homily. Hence, this was his beginning to Lent, which for me is the most important Christian season because of Jesus' crucifixion and resurrection, as nothing else in our faith matters nearly as much. I wondered what the others made of this service, being Catholics and hence used to their overly formal, liturgical style of worship. Many would have come from work, perhaps had not yet had their dinner, being busy in the middle of the week. Thus only 25 minutes devoted to the origins of our faith, bound by Catholic "procedures," with little sense of how fasting and prayers are supposed to help us self-examine our way to greater faith. I did pick up a brochure in the lobby about such introspection, asking many tangential questions, but not the one that matters most: *Who is God, and why should we believe in and serve Him?*

*

What has come to annoy me greatly is our collective assumption that we somehow know who God actually is. It is, of course, easier to say who and what He is not: for me (since I reject the Trinity) God is not human (I would say that Jesus was a God-infused man who transcended into still-human divinity through God's will, though He was not a god on His own), He never dies, He understands everything simultaneously, He continues the Earthen world for our benefit (despite our polluting it, day after decade), and endlessly waits for us to find Him, eventually. God never stops loving us and never quits "doing His job" for us. God is the Father we never deserve but are gifted anyway.

That said, Catholic writer Michael Novak reminded us in one of his books that *no one sees God*, echoing Scripture. This lack of seeing Him fuels even empirical scientists to doubt His presence, as though science can explain the creation and maintenance of the universe without a divine intelligence. Science can describe and explain *what* and *how*, but guesses at *why* less clearly. If the universe was created out of random events, does that mean there is no God, or is it more problematic for them to deal with an unseen Creator? Wiser scientists explain natural events as indicative of God's handiwork, instead of denying Him altogether. Like so much in life, it is not either / or, but both — both what we see in Nature and how the long-unseen complexities (e.g., DNA) were formed out of His wisdom. Astronomers are often telling us about how newly-discovered planets could contain life, but there are so many necessary variables for this to occur. Are we alone in the universe? Probably not, but perhaps we are in our local portion of the Milky Way.

Our prejudices and practices in various religions were formed out of trying to skirt this chasm between our seen world and the unseen God. Jews would say theirs is the only true religion, since it was given to them by God to Abraham and Moses, that no other religions have such momentous ancestors. Muslims would, of course, look to Mohammed in this regard. Christians push this further by citing Jesus Christ as greater than these others, because of His performing miracles and being resurrected. For me, the proof of God comes from the Natural world as well as two main other sources: the Shroud of Turin and near-death experiences, both of which I discussed in my book. Thus, it is not merely faith in the unseen God, but what we see from Him in our lives and establishing Jesus Christ as the bodily linkage between God and ourselves.

So, before and beyond all the religions, limited as they are by substituting doctrines and other systems of thought (e.g., Hinduism) for realistically delving into this fundamental question, let us finally try to better clarify our sense of who God truly is, so late as it is in our human doings:

- We can only assume that God has always existed. Atheists talk about "parallel universes," but this is silly. At some point, He created the universe, perhaps in the "Big Bang" theory as astronomers have described to us. The evolution of the species in the Darwinian manner remains our best means of explaining how humans came to be — not Adam and Eve. God gave we humans free will, thumbs and self-consciousness, allowing us to drift away from Him in abstracted thought, in self-absorbed triumphs and the idolatrous worship of our capacity to make ever-new technology. He knew we could not hold fast to Him in all ways of our being forever, has tolerated our religious factions and frictions, and daily awaits our return to Him. God's patience with us is our constellation. He knew we would eventually shed our primitive awe of His Natural world, and spoil His bounty with our reckless plunder. God likely will not clean up our polluting messes, either, as He tends not to save us from ourselves when we are disobediently foolish.

Whether from some or many of the 300 Old Testament prophecies about the Jewish Messiah or because God knew that we would always partake of idolatry without a physical manifestation of Him, Jesus Christ was born, raised and sacrificed to draw us to God through miracles, teachings and eventually His crucifixion and resurrection to purposefully stifle endless debates about who God might be and how to worship Him. Jesus therefore filled the chasm between the human and the divine with Himself, without doctrines or mere promises for a better life. Jews have generally rejected Jesus because He did not bring world peace, as they had expected. We just finished watching the Winter Olympics, where our expectations are upended almost every day for two weeks. Necessarily, *God does as He wishes*, and it is not for us to second-guess this by overusing doctrines to try explain Him to ourselves.

- Lastly, the old question of why God does so little to ease our lives of burdens, illnesses and death. God never promised to spare us anything, just as He always provides us with the basic Natural elements to sustain us. He might well say that we are too often only ungrateful. He does not attempt to control the weather, to limit the course of illnesses (this has been an especially bad flu season) or prevent tragedies and calamities. God daily provides and occasionally proves Himself to be undeniably miraculous. This may be all we can ask of Him, and thank Him so.

February 2018

WHY THE JEWS HAD TO KILL JESUS

First, about the title. Some will either feel offended or correct me for being historically wrong, since we all know that Jesus was crucified by the Romans. Although I am a Christian, this essay will eventually come around to a Jewish psychological perspective to try to explain the necessity of their removing Him as a problematic influence. This has relevance not only for the ancient Israelites, but also to both subsequent as well as current Jews, who generally still do not accept Jesus as their Messiah. It may also be relevant to atheists, who "kill" Jesus in their disbelief of God, His Father. If we assume that the coming of Jesus was "part of God's plan" for the Jews, He would certainly not be surprised about their rejection of Jesus, as God had a larger idea to forge, that of universal salvation for all people. I will later try to explain why the theological concept of replacement theology (also known as supersessionism) is not quite accurate for what came to occur, since God thinks longer and deeper than we can about what we need from Him.

I will start with my sense of what the Bible tells us about the often strained relationship between Jesus and His fellow Jews. We must always remember that the Gospels were written by four men who wrote at least 30-65 years after Jesus' death and resurrection, and each author had his own interests and biases. For example, in John's Gospel, there is the repeated use of the phrase "the Jews" in a derogatory sense, even though it is likely true that the author was himself a Jew. There are various episodes of Jesus being questioned by the Pharisees, which repeatedly provoke them to want to kill Him. Even His own people in Nazareth are disgruntled enough to want to banish Jesus, who apparently was not always His own best salesman. It seems unlikely that the Romans were problematically knowledgeable about Jesus until during the (third?) Passover that became Holy Week, since they are not mentioned in any accusatory or threatening manner beforehand. What we do not know from the Gospel accounts is whether there were any other provocative statements or actions by or about Jesus that would have garnered the consternation of His own people, besides His actions at the money-changers' tables in the Temple. Even eyewitness testimony can not include everything that happened during Jesus' ministry. As we all know, the Bible is not videotape.

In the Book of Acts, Jesus' followers are also sometimes not safely kept. Stephen gets stoned by other Jews while Saul condones this punishment out of his righteous indignation that any Jews could accept Jesus as their Messiah. Saul's zealotry is curbed only by divine intervention by invoking his temporary blindness but evolving sense that the Gentiles must be included in the Jewish fold. Jewish Law was, if not abandoned, then certainly trimmed as the primary premise for obtaining God's favor. Paul had some luck converting Jews to the new Christian faith, although by the middle of the second century, the schism between Jews and Christians had already hardened. Last year, I read Justin Martyr's *Dialogue With Trypho* (written in ca. 160 CE), which at times almost mocks Judaism in its perceived insufficiency to remain relevant to the Christian cause. Soon enough, Christians largely left the Jews behind as their numbers swelled into the millions within the Roman Empire, as though the two monotheistic groups unwittingly wind up in divorce court with no final settlement beyond the acrimony. There is nothing else like the angst of feeling left behind.

Next, a little bit of history concerning the Israelites, about which I am admittedly too sketchily informed. As some of us learned in Sunday School, they were repeatedly dominated or enslaved over a lengthy period of time: (by) the Pharoah in Egypt, the Assyrians, the Babylonians, the Persians, Alexander the Great, Seleucus, the Romans, and, later on, the Muslims, Christian crusaders and, of course, the Nazis. Jews, understandably, did and do have a persecution complex, about which scholar David Carr writes at length in his fine book, *Holy Resilience* (2014). There is both the history of mistreatment as well as any currently perceived hostilities that have congealed to form a traumatic response style to perceived threats. The current expansion of Israeli settlements is designed to buttress them against Palestinian assaults. Israel is surrounded by other countries seen to be perennially hostile, a reflection of Moses' dilemma prior to the Exodus. This has formed a psychological persona of perpetual victimhood, which, unfortunately, is well deserved. Hitler echoed the late-life anti-Jewish diatribe by Martin Luther to justify rounding up Jews into ghettos and abolishing their rights. This Jewish need to cling to something religiously certain for them in the face of frequent persecution contributed to some of their skepticism against Jesus, an evolving sense of Him as being what Freud called *ego alien* to their traditional Judaism. Jesus thus became *not quite one of them*, a spiritual stranger, ultimately one to be rejected and vanquished.

*

I also want to talk about the psychological necessity of idols. The Old Testament describes the Jews' difficulty with letting go of their idols prior to the Babylonian exile, the best-known being *Baal.* The Egyptians, the Greeks and the Romans, as we know, worshipped a panoply of gods and goddesses over many centuries, and regularly indulged in sacrifices to appease their gods. Being monotheists, we see no need for such sacrifices, and the Jews eventually gave up their idols after the Babylonian exile and their sacrifices after the destruction of their second Temple in 70 CE. What Jews called "the Law" became an intricately detailed written description of what Yahweh could provide and expected from them. Thus, the writing of the Old Testament during and after the Babylonian exile superseded the Jews' need for either idols or sacrifices after the Second Temple was destroyed. They had something else, the Scripture that told stories the idols and the sacrifices could not tell: stories about God and their own people. The Torah and the Talmud became readable "idols," being more specific than stone or wooden objects invested with supernatural influence. You might ask how books can be idols, but then, how is anything else an idol? We invest meaning in all sorts of objects — for example, jewelry, marriage licenses or stop signs. This is one way we are different from other mammals, which can not assign meanings to objects. The Bible as a whole provides a path away from wooden or stone idols toward a readable linkage to God, who is considered to have at least inspired its writing. It is thus more human than idol objects, and certainly we are attracted to reading about ourselves.

By the time Jesus comes along, the Jews' devotion to the Torah (most famously, the 613 laws) had been cemented as, in essence, a religious lifestyle that clearly distinguished them from both the preceding cultures mentioned above as well as their current pests, the Romans, who were still primarily pagans in the old tradition. The Romans tolerated these Jews, but clearly did not understand them, since their gods and goddesses were designed mainly to influence things like the weather or other more impersonal matters. There was no "having a personal relationship" with these gods, nor was there any godly wrath to punish wayward disobedience. The Jews had stepped out of this old tradition because God told Abraham there was a different way, a viable relationship with a divine being. Over the centuries from the Babylonian exile until the time of Jesus, all of this came to be taken for granted by the Jews, that their Scripture had come to form a unique tradition of its own about the world, who created it and what might happen. None of the older traditions had a coherent Genesis story about the creation of the world that people could read, study and even memorize. The Jews had evolved into living idols of their own, internalizing (or, in Freudian language, *introjecting*) God as whom He seemed to be. The Old Testament was a combination of both intricate and broader stories to be nearly worshipped, a commonly-held and shared religious history over a tremendously long period of time. The Jews felt special because God said so, and they fashioned a way of life that highlighted this singular specialness. They still do, visible in synagogues on Fridays or Saturdays every week. Why change what works?

*

Two vignettes in John's Gospel (which is my favorite) illustrate how alarming it becomes for the Jews as Jesus chips away at their tradition. In one instance, other Jews encircle Him to ask "For how long are you going to keep a grip on our soul? If you are the Anointed (the Messiah), tell us forthrightly." To this, Jesus replies "I have told you, and you do not have faith" (10:24-25) In a second instance, other Jews seek to kill Jesus because He not only seemingly breaks the Sabbath, but also "calls God His own Father, making Himself equal to God" (5:18). In these and other instances, Jesus seeks to change what about Judaism, for Him, does not quite work: the mere tenacity of the Law. It is not often mentioned that Jesus only rarely quotes the Old Testament verbatim, but rather alludes to its figures (Abraham, Moses, Isaiah and Noah) when needed. Jesus tells His brethren that He is not a book to be read and studied, He is something more: a direct bodily linkage to God, which they do not think is possible, at least not yet.

Three other well-known Gospel episodes near the end of Jesus' ministry solidify the Jews' resistance to Him, both theologically and even more so psychologically. The examples of healing the blind man, the resurrection of Lazarus in Bethany while Jesus travels to Jerusalem as well as His provocative overturning of the money-changers' tables at the Temple presses His purpose "in their faces" to raise the stakes to ask a basic question: *Who am I to you, and what am I trying to do within our Jewish context?* No one had raised a dead person after four days before, and Jesus used the Temple episode to give the clergy a clear reason to at least arrest Him, sooner than never. I think we blame Judas Iscariot too harshly — he was paid by the clergy to tell them where Jesus was hiding, (perhaps) that is all. Jesus gave the clergy a clear choice between hoarding wealth from "service fees" and accepting His supernatural capacity to affect people outside their domain. Did the

Jews kill Jesus out of their sense of envy that He was closer to God than they were, after ca. 1,800 years?

In addition, there is also the Jewish concept of the Messiah, which has not changed since the time of Jesus, this confirmed by listening to rabbis on YouTube. Their sense of the Messiah is that He could not exist in human form, due to God's divine nature. Our Christian Trinity (which I also do not yet accept) is rejected for the same reason, that God can not be "divided." For Jesus to be crucified by the ugliest death would not befit a Messiah for them. The Jews do not believe in any Second Coming of the Messiah nor Paul's justification by faith. Rather, the Jewish Messiah would usher in both world peace as well as what they call "the ingathering of the exiles," along with the resurrection of *all* of the dead. A third Temple would also be built. Because none of these events have occurred since Jesus' crucifixion, our Christian sense of the Messiah is rejected by the Jews. Obviously, this concept comes to the fore after Jesus dies and is resurrected (the latter of which is also dismissed by His brethren), yet, because His body is never found, a seed of doubt as to their sense of the Messiah is planted, allowing some Jews to accept Jesus for the next hundred or so years. I will discuss the current phenomenon of Messianic Jews a little later, as perhaps they are the way to answer the question Christians always want to ask the Jews, namely, "Where is your Messiah, after nearly 2,000 years?" I don't think God expected them to have to wait quite so long.

For brevity's sake, I will link together the general Jewish responses to Jesus and the Apostles as well as Paul, Stephen and subsequent early Christians. What Jesus rarely mentions and Paul eventually sets aside altogether are the basic tenets of the Jewish faith. In Jesus' case, He assumes this is common knowledge and practice, in Paul's case because not only has Jesus not emphasized what is already well-known, but because he understands where Jesus is going, as it happened to him. Paul was stopped literally in the middle of the road, temporarily blinded and transformed. Jesus told Paul what he was to do, pushing him far beyond what Paul had understood about his cherished Judaism, which, ironically, would get him into much trouble with the very brethren who once respected him. Jesus never does this to any other fellow Jews, either individually or collectively. Rather, He is merely disbelieved and ultimately disowned by His own people. I think what Jesus is telling them is *our Judaism is not enough, it is too narrow and even idol-prone in its tenacious preoccupation with how we think God works in our world.* Jesus tries to push them out toward the edges of where Judaism meets God (whom He knows), but they resist this "suggested journey of faith." That this occurs repeatedly over several years, whether within his own community in Nazareth or in Jerusalem, renders Him as *ego alien* to other Jews, meaning *You are not one of us anymore.* In social psychology, it is the one who perturbs the group to which (s)he belongs that requires the most certain expulsion. It could be said that it was the Jews and not the Catholics who invented ex-communication, since Jesus became intolerable as one of their own. If Jesus were a member of the Mafia who, under threat of lengthy imprisonment, told the police all he knew about their organization, they would want to kill him. We hate those who have belonged to us and later turn against us. The Pharisees and Sadducees envied not only Jesus' popularity amongst the common Jewish people, but they also envied his wisdom, His many miracles and His apparent direct connection with the God they had labored to serve for so many centuries. Intense envy can make men do things they would not otherwise do. That Paul was later beheaded and nearly all the Apostles were martyred by fellow Jews is our Christian tragedy, but a Jewish necessity.

There is also the psychological impact of martyrdom, both after the death of Jesus as well as the Apostles (most of whom were apparently martyred) and others later on. God would well understand how martyrdom would influence both the Apostles and later followers, but, more importantly, He would know that this would provide a lingering sentiment for subsequent generations. Scholar Bart Ehrman, in his new book, *The Triumph of Christianity*, attributes the explosive growth of the Christian faith over the first several centuries in part to persistent miracles, to which I would add the not-so-subtle impact of martyrdom. I am not sure whether other Jews would be that familiar with martyrdom in individual cases, but they would certainly understand collective suffering for their faith, from Egypt onward. Christians wear crosses as an introjection of what we could never witness: the martyred suffering of Jesus, which still reaches us, at least at Eastertime, all these years later. For those of you who are familiar with medical aspects of crucifixion or the Shroud of Turin, this may be the fountainhead of Christian introjection, when even Scripture dropped away and Jesus became only the Son of God.

*

So, what am I saying? I am saying that Jesus over years stretched Judaism to nearly the breaking-point, not that it would cease to exist bur rather to where it might travel beyond merely laws and culture. He was not telling his brethren to reject their faith, but to supplement it with a more expansive sense of purpose. Thus, He was advocating religious addition and not subtraction, though Jesus was rejected by their lack of Spiritual geometry, being unable to traverse the human to truly find the divine. They rejected Jesus as a turncoat, not quite a false prophet, but someone whom they could not comprehend, either theologically or psychologically, breeding intensely hostile envious resistance. I am speaking mostly of the Jewish clergy, and not the common people, who tended to find Jesus to be a curiosity, if not more. Once Jesus was gone, subsequent generations had no literal figure to consider, and most people had no Gospels to read — rather it became all word-of-mouth, which I think handicapped Paul with his fellow Jews. They had the Torah and all he had was his own transformative blindness. I often think of the title of a book I read several years ago, namely, *No One Sees God.*

I am not talking about replacement theology as some sort of "Christian improvement" on Judaism — it is not about trading one model for another of the same brand of car. If Jesus were a snake that shed its skin, He would still be a snake. Christian faith is an outgrowth of Judaism, and would not exist without it. We Christians are given too little Jewish history, and are biased against Jews for killing Jesus, even now, despite ongoing ecumenical efforts since the Catholic Church worked to mend fences fifty years ago. Atheists "kill" God (and hence Jesus) because they can not find Him, and are angry because He does not readily explain Himself to we impatient humans. As I discussed in my own book, *Once Every Day Becomes Easter* (2015), the perpetual gap between the human and the divine never really shrinks, until and unless God surprises us with a fresh and undeniable example of Himself. Messianic Jews found Jesus over the past 45 years by finally reading the New Testament but keeping their Judaism intact. Apparently they are not always treated so kindly in Israel.

Finally, for me what really matters is how well or poorly each and all of us can introject God and Jesus into some kind of working muscular faith. Any religion can provide useful material and ideas to aid our efforts, though I can't say all religions are of equal value to me, or even denominations within Christianity. It is not that all or none suit me, nor does "post-denominational" quite suit either, since we all have unproven biases about God. If there was an announced death of theology, regardless of the religion, I might well clap more than a little over that. God is who He is, and all our theology will never affect that, not even once. It is our Spiritual task to pull Him inside us and keep Him there, for as often and as long as we can. Always remember: *God, through Judaism, gave us Jesus.*

July 2018

ALL THAT GOD ALLOWS

I am writing this shortly after two major hurricanes have ripped through both my adopted state of North Carolina as well as Florida and Georgia. These hurricanes have flooded or destroyed homes in North Carolina and flattened entire towns in coastal Florida. As always, there were personal stories both of people who either dodged tragedy or who were injured or killed unmercifully. As always, I was struck by how God was to be understood as "He who saved us," but never "He who let some of us die." We are often afraid to allow God to let bad things happen to good (or bad) people, because we are afraid it might mean that He does not truly love and care about us.

Examples of weather disasters or, more commonly, illnesses such as cancer, perplex those who do (and don't) believe in God because it seems that He is either disinterested in our personal welfare or somehow doesn't bother to intervene when he "clearly should." When there is a welcomed medical recovery or someone survives a hurricane, we can be quick to praise God's mercy, when it can be merely fortuitous. If my house remains intact and my neighbor's house gets damaged or destroyed in a tornado, should I praise God while (s)he curses Him? Such examples and many others point to that old nagging question for anyone of any faith: *(How) does God intervene in our lives in ways that we can know it is Him, and not either luck or "fate?"* God's miracles are obvious.

I want to try to answer this and corollary questions because it is as old as the ancient Israelites, who impatiently yearned for their Messiah in the century before Jesus was born, asking God to be relieved of persecution and poverty, which had dogged them from the beginning. The Genesis story, for me, is the Jewish effort to make sense of God as both Creator and intervener as well as to understand our human frailty and sinfulness. The Adam and Eve story immediately exposes the gap between God and ourselves, between the human and the divine, and how to make any sense of His importance for us. It is always tempting to take up the deist position: that God created the world and will spend the rest of time reading, watching television or, worse, sleeping. Atheists shout that the universe is a random assortment of events, crises and deaths with no discernable patterns or reasons for anything that occurs, whether useful or terrible. It is also tempting to adopt this position because, ironically, it lets God off the hook: *what is His real involvement with us, anyway*? I do sense that He is always watching everything, and so is not asleep. To even suppose that God sleeps at all is merely human in the first place.

*

I am more than ambivalent about theology because of its tendency to allow our human speculations about God to harden into many sorts of doctrine, as though this actually makes any greater sense. Ascribing "God's hand" to the above circumstances might not seem like theology, but it often is — it is "layman's theology" to try to make sense of what happens to us. In the above example, it is unlikely that God both exerts His influence to save my house but to allow my neighbor's house to be ruined. Any such sentiments are speculative because there is no clearly discernable "proof" that God affects either of our houses. To be silly, if my neighbor's house was destroyed and was then mysteriously rebuilt during the night, we would all call that God's miraculous work and praise Him accordingly. We would *know* that God had "stepped in to right things."

So I start with the most basic of questions: *How do we know when God (in)directly influences our lives beyond speculation or coincidence?* How do we know when it is really Him and not something else more explicable? I will necessarily reject John Calvin's (16th Century Reformation theologian who broke with Catholicism) notion of God as "worldly micro-manager," who resisted our having any viable free will, and who doubted that most of us could be accepted by God because of our inherent human "depravity." Calvin took Augustine's notion of original sin to the nearly the extreme, and generally also objected to chance or coincidence, believing that God controlled (nearly) everything. Rather, I will argue the opposite: that God allows for much to happen in our world without His (in)direct influence, to the point that could, in atheistic hands, push God so far to the periphery that He nearly ceases to matter. *How does God truly matter?*

I want to take the opposite approach from theology: not so much guessing, and look at God from His perspective instead. If theology is only human speculation, what does God's influence look like for us? I will posit that not only is there free will, but there may be *too much* of it, meaning that *we* allow or control so much of what goes on in our world, and the rest may well no longer function under God's immediate, day-to-day influence. If we say that God created the means for the evolution of the species after the Earth cooled and formed its early readiness for such life, that, of course, belongs to God. We could not create the world on our own, nor is it randomly created. There are many variables which have to line up quite closely for life as we understand it to exist at all — having a moon, for example. So God made the process by which weather occurs, the ocean tides, the four natural elements, gravity, photosynthesis and so on. I don't know that He actively controls this even on a seasonal basis, but, as Catholic biologist Kenneth Miller argues, God set all of this in motion "in the beginning." That is the real Genesis story. I do not believe that He controls the daily temperatures where we live, whether it rains (sorry) or whether there are storms or droughts, because, unlike both Jewish and certain Christian thought, I do not believe that God intentionally punishes us, even for our worst sins. I don't know that He created the world with us fully in mind at all — which is unanswerable — even for those who accept the Trinity. We came along very late, and probably not without at least some hesitation on God's part, being who and what we are.

*

So, if we could not have created our world, God does not intentionally punish us and there may be too much human free will, where does that leave us in terms of more clearly recognizing the will of God in our world? In the Adam and Eve story, they succumb to temptation and God banishes them from paradise, but what is this "tree of knowledge?" It defines the gap between the human and the divine, it defines how easily we are "relieved" of God to follow our own ways, and, yes, they were naked. Is sex part of the "tree of knowledge?" Yes, it is. This Jewish mythological story's impetus is to define the price we pay for disobeying God by exercising our God-given free human will to disobey Him. None of the other creatures in the animal kingdom have this "problem," as God has biologically "programmed" them to avoid straying into sin, coupled with a lack of sufficient abstract reasoning. Thus, we are "stuck" with our "intelligent" free will as humans, I don't think God has ever punished us for it (since He gave it to us, just like sexual orgasm), and so what He really wants is for us to keep returning to the garden, which is to find Him again and again until He is pulled inside us enough to affect (some of) what we say and do, what Freud called *introjection*. All of which is to say that what God mostly does with us is to watch, listen and wait for if and when He wants to intervene in our lives. This, of course, frustrates us to no end, since He "should want to intervene in our lives all the time, each and every day." That's His job, right? Well, yes.

I have written previously about how God could have stopped with the other animals and never created we humans, and saved Himself a lot of anguish. God has suffered far more anguish from all of us than in poor Job's story, and it all really happens, every day. God has daily bouts of anguish, likely has doubts about creating us in the first place, yet He remains perpetually patient for our finding Him again. He never sleeps and He is forever patient. As I wrote in a poem several years ago, *God's patience is our constellation*. So I begin to answer the question with what is obvious: since each of us has free will, collectively God does nothing to intervene against our will, because He gave it to us permissibly. Just like the weather, He does not attempt to control us at all. Rather, He waits for when to intervene, which, for us, is far too seldom. This is not Deism, however. As I believe in miracles, there can be no Deism, since God is not reading or watching television, rather He surgically presents Himself at the necessary time and place, performs His miracles, and we all know it for what they are. Surgeons in particular have described how some operations turn out well despite what seems like the certain death of the patient, and people recover miraculously. People have heart attacks and are clinically dead for most of one hour or more and survive, without brain damage. Almost any physician will tell you they know when God intervenes with their patients, it is inexplicable otherwise. They are saying *Don't tell us there is no God, we know better.* So, there is free human will and there are Godly miracles — the human and divine, not directly linked yet acutely and situationally inseparable.

Secondly, I want to take up the old question of why God lets us suffer. Adam and Eve "suffer" through banishment from Eden in provoking God's wrath at their sinful temptation. I don't believe in God's wrath, however, as, beyond Old Testament stories, I see no evidence for it. The notion of the wrath of God is a human one, not His. The same is true for Hell, I don't see much evidence for it beyond the occasional story. People have repeatedly visited Heaven for centuries, and find only His Fatherly love there. But yes, God will let us suffer, whether medically, psychologically or even spiritually.

Lately, I have been reading about the early Christian martyrs. Although scholars generally now think that the sheer amount of persecution by the Romans was probably exaggerated, there is no question that during what is known as "the Great Persecution" (303-313 CE) that Christians died in significant numbers from barbarously ill treatment. Some of them literally "died for God" in refusing to recant their Christian faith by performing sacrifices for the Romans' pagan gods, as had become decreed by their emperor. While these martyrs probably expected to go to Heaven, this is still quite an example of introjection and suffering. God never told them to die for Him, that was their necessity, and some martyrs became cherished by the early Catholic church.

Why does God let tragedies and calamities happen, and why does He let us suffer? Because He allows the world to happen as it does, which includes joy as well as suffering. Suffering is the price of our being alive, this is what some of the early theologians said, based on Jesus' crucifixion and these martyrs. By being alive, we can receive the best and worst, and everything else in between. Sometimes or perhaps many times, God does not answer our prayers about our situations because (I think) He sees this as what necessarily occurs in life. He does not spare us anymore than He spared Jesus, His only Son, on the Cross. Jesus, in reciting the beginning of Psalm 22, felt abandoned by God, and, after such calamities as cancer or hurricanes, so can we. We hurt when God does not spare us, and often, He does not. For those who are familiar with near-death experiences (NDEs), it is God who decides to perform medical miracles in usually emergency situations, often in response to intense familial petitions of prayer. He can let us suffer or He can miraculously heal us, it is always His choice. Most of the time, God lets us suffer. The English physicist Stephen Hawking died earlier this year with the atheistic sentiment that there is no God. He contracted ALS, a neuro-muscular disease, at age 21 and died at age 76 (the longest-known surviving ALS patient), spending the rest of his life in a wheelchair, unable to speak. It is understandable that he would not believe in God, but that does not mean God does not exist. There is the ripe beauty of the Natural world, the holy temple of the human body, sexual orgasm and love, and there is sickness and death. It is a package deal. Even people who have made suicide attempts have had NDEs. God's "mysterious ways" are indeed that — His and His alone.

All of this likely feels depressing, and it is when illness or tragedy affects any or all of us. It can feel random and lacerating, this life of ours. It is also righteously joyous, and sometimes we at least glimpse semblances of the divine. God makes no promises to anyone of us beyond giving us the chance to be alive. Since we didn't create ourselves, that must be enough. It doesn't make Him unnecessary or irrelevant. *No one sees God*, I try to remember, yet He hovers, waits, anguishes and intervenes, just like we do. One day, Heaven awaits most or all of us in some "fourth dimension" of space and time where everyone is alive again, so say those who have visited there. I hope so. For some or many of us, the relief will prove immeasurable. God always awaits us, everlastingly patient.

October 2018

THE TREMOROUS INVISIBILITY OF GOD

After reading Michael Novak's book, *No One Sees God* (2008) several years ago, as much as I enjoyed the book, it has been its title that has stuck most with me, the clear simplicity of this most vexing aspect of God: His invisibility. It forms the basis for all of our various religious ideas, doctrines, practices and even superstitions. It floods the vacuum between the human and the divine, as though a huge veil hides all of God's love, mercy and "works" (particularly miracles) from our view, which only prods us to speculate about Him through "rumors" and ideas, which may well be quite off the mark. God's invisibility becomes clearest in the times of our personal and collective spiritual angst, when we harken skyward to be answered by He who knows all, but shares such too sparingly. And so, for thousands of years, we have sometimes foolishly filled in this vacuum with our own, too-human, remedies.

For a very long time, the primitives had simple rituals about God's invisibility, centered around their quite Naturalized sense of the world, with only limited speculation, there being no real theology. Theology is our human speculation about how God functions, upon which religious practices are formed and passed down through the generations as though they are accurate and necessary. I would say that, too often, they are not, and actually set us apart from God by imposing what fills this human-divine vacuum with too many and often too-complex notions of "how God is." This is true regardless of the religion involved, and indeed, is common to virtually every "evolving" religion. I would say that religion itself is designed to deal with this invisibility of God in the form of the human-divine vacuum, and, too often, fails to satisfactorily straddle this perhaps unshrinkable chasm with the bloated speculation of the well-meaning but likely wrong. The old refrain is *"God only knows."*

*

It occurred to me that a relevant starting point for looking closer at God's invisibility would be to discuss the long history of animal sacrifices in various religions. It is thought that, as peoples became more agrarian, such sacrifices showed appreciation to the gods for bountiful harvests. A long list of cultures involved in such sacrifices include: the Egyptians, Canaanites, Minoans, Persians, Hebrews (early Jews), Greeks, Romans as well as present-day Islam and Hinduism. All such cultures invented intricate practices for their animal sacrifices, which, for the Israelites, for example, perhaps led to their complex dietary laws over time. Common to such practices was that the animals needed to be "unblemished" in order to atone for our human sins as offered to the relevant gods as a kind of sacrifice-induced forgiveness, or at least thanking them for good fortune. These rituals of animal sacrifices would be organized around our speculation about what the gods demanded from us in exchange for either divine benevolence or to forestall their wrath. Long before there was the sophisticated organization of either Judaism or Christianity (the religions with which we are most familiar), these animal sacrifices formed the basis for our attempts to both explain and possibly shrink the human-divine chasm in ways that were sensible and could sustain us through both successes and calamities. *The problem is, they don't really work.* After the destruction of the second Jewish temple in 70 C.E., these sacrifices ended, and have never resumed. The word *holocaust* means "burnt offering." Christians would say that Jesus was our sacrifice that superseded the animals, even though there were occasions of other human sacrifices, and not just the virgins in old stories. We proud modern-types would say that we are long past needing animal sacrifices to worship God, but what about His invisibility?

In replacing these animal sacrifices, there came the Jewish ideas about cleanliness and foregoing idol worship, combined with liturgical worship in the synagogues, which would later profoundly influence

Catholic and, to a lesser extent, Protestant church services. Out of Torah observance would come Jesus' Lord's Prayer and later the Apostles' and Nicene Creeds, the latter heralding the notion of "beliefs" as a means of clarifying how we could sight God on our side of the human-divine chasm, whether or not this suited Him or reflected "His ways." It would be these beliefs that would spur the permanent rift between Jews and Christians, much later between Catholics and Protestants, and still later the often misguided denominational friction within the Protestant churches. God had become the subject of innumerable doctrinal disputes, about which He would likely snicker, saying to us: *I never made you to have foolish disputes about Me, since I know better.* Dietary laws, liturgies and creeds were formulated to plug some of the many holes that are the human-divine vacuum, but they tend to leak and even disappear once we step outside of our churches into the larger world. I discussed my objections to the Holy Trinity in a previous essay. Communion (or the Eucharist), coming from Jesus Himself, functions as a direct expression of what God wants from us as worship of Him. It is edibly and drinkably tangible compared to the abstraction of baptism, just as the 23rd Psalm, in its plaintive brevity, sings above the more wailsome prose of many of the other Psalms. Religion has always been about what we can hold onto between weekly worship services. So we ask: *How do we continually conjure and serve He whom we can not see?*

*

What is the role of prayer in trying to alleviate God's invisibility? It is through prayer that any or all of what church-goers take from religious services to personalize into voicing our needs on a daily basis. When spoken in church, the calling of "Let us pray" is quickly drawn into often-familiar verbiage which bypasses the most vexing question: *Who is God, and what might He look like? Or, who is it that we are praying to*? This issue of our inability to see God's "face," to my recollection of many years spent in churches, is never articulated, and probably would be described as "Whoever God looks like to each of you." The chronic weight of churched familiarity sometimes dissolves completely when we are praying to God on our own. We become more acutely aware of the human-divine chasm, and sometimes "the words do not come" or what has been called "dry prayers." When I first started writing religious poetry over 30 years ago, I conjured God's face as having 12 eyes, one for each of the hours of the daytime or night-time, meaning that He had panoptical sight, being able to see in all directions at once. I no longer pray to what I perceive as God's "maybe face," since I now know that anything I might conjure would undoubtedly be wrong. Theology is unintentionally designed to diminish our helplessness before God out of knowing so little about Him. It gives us a false sense of confidence, which too easily melts before the reality of how ignorant about Him we actually are. It is during prayer that such ignorant helplessness becomes apparent to most of us, whether seldom or overly often. It then becomes easier to turn away from God, saying "I'll come back to You tomorrow." Not being Catholic, I am not interested in reciting rote devotional prayers offered by that church, because I believe God wants us to come unto Him "as we are," not through rehearsed, sanctioned prayers nearly trademarked and overly familiar. God wants to be "beseeched," not merely "talked to." He hears millions or billions of prayers each day, I think He has an "ego," and wants to be addressed sincerely. Whether He has become jaded about our prayer-making after so many years of attempts to influence Him, we can't know.

We can not make God visible, that is our problem, regardless of whichever religion or not. Nothing learned in or out of church changes this inevitability, and it is we who must accept or reject Him on this basis. Having chatted with atheists on the Internet, it became clear to me that it is God's invisibility they are rejecting as a "problem" with which to wrestle, rather than only their tired "science and logic" arguments. Since Jesus was the only person who, with God's help, straddled the human-divine chasm, we barely have any clear sense of

His actual face, much less God's. What we are being asked to do, both through prayer as well as acts of service unto others, is to accept being guided by an unseeable force of Nature beyond any real capacity to comprehend Him, unless through the miraculous. The Trinity may well have been inspired by the sense that Jesus is as close as we are going to get to what God is like. Clearly, He is God's human representation on earth. Judaism says the Messiah is necessarily human, and nothing more. Christians accept that God infused Himself through Jesus to show us what is "Godly possible," what emanates from a place called Heaven. Jesus became the solution to idol worship, though even He was killed. We are all self-referential.

*

So, what do I mean by *tremorous*? If we accept the phenomenon of a human-divine chasm (which, to me, is indisputable), there will be times when our experiences of this chasm induces what I will call "the anxiety over sighting God" as a divine intervener in our lives. Medical emergencies come immediately to mind, particularly those that are deemed "life and death." We can forget about God until He urgently matters, then we no longer care what He looks like — we just want Him to help our loved ones in need. We turn our own faces back toward Him in the shameless expectancy of aid, however wayward we had been, even the day before, seeking tremors of whether God will answer our beseeching prayers well and soon enough to matter. We ourselves momentarily straddle that chasm, nearly demanding to be heard by our unseeable and untouchable Father, who knows everything and from whom "nothing is impossible." For God to be mercy-fully forthcoming with His love and divine powers. These are tremors of our unyielding needs.

There are also the tremors of sensing that nothing is coming, that God is either disinterested or unwilling to grant our wishes, that He will "say NO again," that we are only talking to the air or He has better people to consider. Not all prayers nor most prayers will be granted, so why are we asking? Tremors from Scripture or churches telling us that our prayers will be granted, Jesus Himself saying so. Tremors over what to say to God or whether He will release Himself into our lives — what everyone calls "the old doubts," since He works more than a little differently from us. Tremors that there really is no God at all, that we have been fooling ourselves since the Jews found their monotheistic God perhaps 4,000 years ago in the desert. Tremors about what a "relationship with God" really is, since it is not clearly reciprocal, and how can we have a relationship with a "ghost?"

If I sound doubt-full about God, I am not, even though I have yet to be blessed by Him from my own prayer-full petitions, because I have come to know a little more about how He actually works. *God was never human.* A slippery relationship with Him at best, until He truly comes, then everything changes and all our doubts die. If we do not see this in our lives, we see it in others. We saw it Jesus' own life. It is Lent as I write, and we all know what is coming: Jesus' bloody death and transcendent radiance in the tomb. Our tremors can die, too. Amen.

March 2019

WHY WE LEAVE THE CLERGY BEHIND

I am writing this in response to reading Episcopalian priest Fleming Rutledge's book, *The Crucifixion* (2015), which has received many accolades, including *Christianity Today's* Book of the Year in 2017 as well as rave reviews on Amazon. It is seen by the clergy as a lengthy (612 pages) summation of Christian theological exploration of Jesus' crucifixion in terms of its primarily Scriptural meanings and how this presumably makes this occurrence a singular event in better defining God's intent in our world. I wish I could share others' enthusiasm for this admittedly hefty and valuable undertaking, but I do not. While the book is well-written and covers much relevant territory, it does so in an overly antiquated manner, removed from both psychology and the Resurrection itself. I will respond to aspects of the book which bristle me as the book proceeds, quoting at times and offering my own perspective. I then want to come around to how this sort of traditional "preaching through a book" can leave lay people with the sense that Jesus' crucifixion and resurrection can only be understood by those whom He called "the learned and the wise," due to the theological complexity involved.

I will start with where I agree with Rutledge. She plainly states "the crucifixion is the most important historical event that has ever happened," which, in a Spiritual sense, is true, and that it serves as "the touchstone of Christian authenticity" (both: p.44). To her credit, Rutledge spends a *few* pages describing the crucifixion's medical details (of which most clergy are overly unfamiliar), but then almost dismisses this in favor of theological interpretations. For example, she says "Christ's blood is a metaphor" (p. 283). No, Christ's blood is type AB (universal donor), its loss contributed to His death by cardio-vascular shock, is clearly seen on the Shroud of Turin, and so is no "metaphor." Being a strong advocate of the Trinity, Rutledge describes Jesus as "God disguised as a man" (p. 62), which I can accept despite my disavowing the Trinity, described elsewhere on this website at length. Rutledge contradicts herself by describing the medical aspects of the crucifixion, but then claims "we must to some degree set it all aside" (p. 96) in favor of voluminous theological speculation, with which I strenuously disagree. All the theology in the world will never explain what actually happened in the tomb, and I would expect her to understand this so late in our Christian journey. The terror of Jesus' suffering is completely unimaginable to anyone who has not at least witnessed crucifixion first hand, much less experienced it. What I do generally admire is that Rutledge takes up the crucifixion as being central to our faith — I just don't like enough of how she does so.

A chapter about individual and social justice resonates with familiar verses from the Old Testament before coming around to the slippery subjects of forgiveness and reconciliation, with recent examples from world events described. Underlying this is Rutledge's unwavering fondness for John Calvin, the 16th Century Reformation thinker who single-handedly created the later oppressive Puritan movement in Britain and America, which imploded with the Salem witch trials. She states: "From beginning to end, the Holy Scriptures testify that the predicament of fallen humanity is so serious, so grave, so irremediable from within, that nothing short of divine intervention can rectify it" (p. 127). Yet out of this Calvinist pessimism comes her effort to describe viable forgiveness by admitting "it (forgiveness) is not a simple matter" (p.131). I wrote a chapter on the psychological aspects of forgiveness in my own book, *Once Every Day Becomes Easter* (2015), which looks at this subject as reflective of the personal need to heal from translating others' offense(s) unto us into something comprehensible, while expecting remorse, when possible. Forgiveness can take months or years, and, in some cases, never happens. Even Jesus, in his allusion to Daniel's "seventy times seven," is too simple. Forgiveness can be long work, indeed.

After justice and forgiveness comes "the gravity of sin," which Rutledge explains is "an exclusively Biblical concept" in which we are "catastrophically separated from the eternal love of God" (p.174), which I would describe as willful transgressions against God's preferences. She says we are "helplessly trapped inside one's own worst self" because of "an active, malevolent agency bent upon despoiling, imprisonment and death" (p.175). Rutledge is, of course, alluding to Satan or the Devil (as does Pope Francis on occasion), which I reject as a long outdated concept, even if Jesus believed in such a figure. His crucifixion was designed by God to relieve our sins, but this never actually happens. If He "took away the sins of the world," why is our world in such tough shape in so many ways? Rutledge's later lengthy discussion of atonement does not adequately explain the necessity of rendering Jesus in the flesh. His primary purpose was to *make God visible to us*. Adam and Eve are invoked as the Jews' mythological explanation for the origins of sin, that is then inexplicably passed across generations forever. If babies are born sinful, then Christianity was a mistake. She describes the Israelites' use of animal sacrifices (to me, a pagan concept, since animals have no inherent Spiritual value) as necessary due to this chasm between the divine God and our own sinfulness. From Hebrews 9:22: "Without the shedding of blood, there is no forgiveness of sins," which, for me, is dogmatically useless in any transcendent religion. Judaism itself gave up animal sacrifices after the second Temple was destroyed by the Romans in 70 C.E. Our ability to both acknowledge and express guilt or remorse as well as make amends to those we have wronged is entirely dependent upon our capacity to be honest with ourselves, which is, again, a psychological process. To be "enslaved" by sin comes not from any Devil, but from what Freud would have called "ego-syntonic wishes." Here, Rutledge's old-school theology is positively archaic, and she lives too much in a tattered "Bible bubble," chewing on rather ancient stuff. Psychology nearly always trumps theology.

There are momentary statements made by Rutledge that chafe me beyond a chapter on God's verses our own judgment (ours tends to win out), such as "faith is not a work" (p.331), which too simply describes the actual conversion process, which can, like forgiveness, take months or years. "Only God is charge of the future" (p.336) — well, yes and no, depending on what we are talking about. Jesus' supposed "descent into Hell" comes from the Apostles' Creed, and not anything historically confirmed. Later on, Rutledge admits that "John Calvin has acquired an undeservedly bad name among many in the churches" (p. 483). No, it is a well-deserved reputation. Calvin's calling people "depraved worms" and deciding that only a relative few can get to Heaven no matter what they do (predestination) would make Calvin wiser than God Himself. We have accounts of near-death experiences from both atheists and suicidal people which discount this notion. Only God decides who enters Heaven, that is true, but who does get there can surprise us. The last third of the book is less interesting, to the point of allowing mild skimming. Despite Rutledge not being a Biblical scholar per se, she borrows much from scholars (e.g., Karl Barth), to the point that her own personal contribution becomes a little suspect. Not plagiarism, just a lack of new ideas. I wish there was more revelation in such a lengthy, clearly important-to-her book. While *The Crucifixion* was worth reading because its subject is intrinsically so central to our Christian faith, I will not be keeping it on my bookshelf. I would instead recommend more highly a book about the little-discussed subject of Holy Saturday by the late Alan Lewis, entitled *Between Cross and Resurrection* (2001). Rutledge initially alludes to the intricate relationship between these two events, but never clearly mentions their kinship again.

*

So what does this book say about both the usefulness of Christian theology and the current state of our church, given its generally glowing reviews? I do admire Rutledge's dogged determination to push Jesus' crucifixion back to the forefront of our interest, but her effort winds up being overly abstract and secondary to the terrorable physicality of the resurrection. Could the impetus of her book be honed into even a series of, say, half-hour sermons, since she was a pastor for many years?

Our problem is multi-fold. As someone has said: how could we translate the miraculous event of the resurrection for those who came later and thus could not witness it? Unfortunately, the answer, by the mid-third century, was theology. We had Justin Martyr, (*Dialog With Trypho*), Tertullian (who coined the term *trinitas*) and Augustine (who misinterpreted his high sex drive as sinful, and became celibate), which led to the formation of the Catholic church, which has always prized theology over (especially) biological reality. As I wrote in an essay earlier this year, the real problem that all we religious people face, regardless of which faith or denomination, is God's invisibility. It is a kind of black hole, into which much of our scholarly and pastoral energy has been poured to elucidate His meaning and purpose. Theology can be useful when it is not unnecessarily complex and speculative, but we always have to remember that it is slippery business: prone to being at least half-wrong, and generally does not truly affect the spirituality of most people. The clergy would say that theology is for themselves, much like doctors and lawyers have "their own language." But medicine and the law are not God or Jesus, they can be seen and felt. Rutledge's quasi-obsession is to correct theology about the crucifixion, but what does this give the rest of us who are not of the clergy? The "problem" of God's invisibility is not going to primarily be solved by our speculative theology, no matter how intricate or repetitively improved it becomes. Any astronomer will tell us that their theories about whichever aspects of the universe will certainly be altered by telescopes and satellites. The clergy has no such help, so what to do? Rutledge, like most Biblical scholars or the clergy, tends to shy away from speculating about the resurrection, and too many of them are unfamiliar with forty years of research on the Shroud of Turin, which is what brought me back to God from the heathen wilderness. On any day, I can see God's divinity, beyond the Bible and theology. Jesus looks out at us, facially asking: *How else would you explain this?*

People, like myself, are leaving the church because of excessive admiration for books like Rutledge's, because they substitute for what needs to go on in church: greater clarity about the relevance of God and Jesus, not the finer points of some academics' theological pontifications. The church has stagnated during my lifetime, seems to be floating in the aether, and thus has to find itself before Millennials take over the world. Rutledge's book, unfortunately, does not sufficiently aid that cause, which is a shame, because its subject matter, to paraphrase Pope Benedict, is nearly everything.

May 2019

CHRISTIANITY HAS GOTTEN STUCK

One of my interests has become to look at the state of our Christian faith, not merely that of the Church, but, more broadly, its state in the larger context of Western society. Most keenly, how is Christianity working, both as personal faith as well as in our culture at large. We are at a crossroads between the Christian tradition as fostered by the Church and the much-discussed decline of congregational attendance and the mild uprising of atheism in America and Britain, in particular, in recent years. It has become quite clear that the Church tradition of many centuries, especially in the 20th Century, is less sustainable now than at any point in my lifetime. Young people are wary of the Church for different reasons, and so are reluctant to join its "system," thus incurring continued declining attendance and involvement. Statistics abound about this decline, some even stating openly that the Church will never recover a sustaining level of attendance. Churches are sold every day to become other businesses entirely, such as restaurants.

Beyond the "Church crisis" is the larger question of what is the place of spiritual persuasion in a heavily secular society which values science over hints of the supernatural. I could ask *Should we believe in God any longer*, but my bias is clearly that we should and must, because there is no more viable alternative. One of worst false dichotomies is between science and religion, which I will not belabor here.

Rather than to range too far and risk addressing nothing clearly, I want to look at three groups which, in combination, grind toward an inertia which slowly threatens the vitality of Christianity, each for its own reasons. These are: 1) the generally stullifying nature of the Christian clergy, regardless of denomination; 2) the continued objections of Jews to accepting Jesus as their Messiah; and 3) the up-risen nuisance that is atheism, which I liken to a nagging parasitic infestation that can be ignored, but not without some consequence, particularly to gullible younger, well-educated men.

*

The clergy are, of course, trained in seminaries. They learn about Scripture and its exegesis, used frequently in sermons that buttress Lectionary passages. While this is designed to educate congregations, I generally found this style to be meandering at best and boring at worst. Clergy learn about the history of the Church, although this is rarely presented either coherently or in depth during services or in Sunday school. Seminaries provide education for clergy the way the military provides training for soldiers: the only way. There is some skepticism from theology professors about the veracity of Gospel material, but students do not seem to be encouraged to think for themselves meaningfully. Over the many years that I attended three churches, little sustained me from the pulpit, despite being exposed to many different preachers. My involvement with Sunday School classes brought no real enlightenment, and, indeed, at least in my own experience, the clergy tended to not actually teach such classes. While each clergy-person is unique, what they express in the tradition of the Church remains more similar than different. This is understandable, and yet unfortunate. My sense is that most clergy, especially the Catholic clergy, are clinging to a Church tradition which has become slippery, and their fear of lack of sustained employment is justified. These people work very hard, but, all too often, are not accomplishing nearly enough. People leave the Church because of what I have called "the monotony of performances," the same thing every week and every year, seemingly forever. The clergy are perhaps the only professionally trained people who are getting rejected as a profession by so many people, compared to doctors, dentists, lawyers and others. I heard one preacher admit from the pulpit that her seminary education had not prepared her for the reality of the 21st Century church situation, which has greater ramifications for their profession because it is not as easy to either teach themselves or find alternative mentors. To a greater extent, the clergy are a hall of mirrors, with no clear path toward anything new and valuable.

My suggestions would be for the clergy to look *very hard* at their situation, and ask, for them, the less obvious question: *Why should people still go to church?* What can one or two hours a week provide in that setting what can not be obtained elsewhere? People do not go to church merely to serve on committees. The clergy needs to abandon the Lectionary system as a mainstay process, and teach what they feel their congregations need. Broader brush strokes of Scripture or relevant Church history would be useful. Taking up moral questions would certainly be appreciated. Better quality sermons couldn't hurt, preferably unwritten. since Jesus never wrote anything down. Simplifying and diversifying the basic church service would be another option to relieve monotony. What appeals to me is an opening hymn, then the first half of a two-part sermon, a second hymn while the offering is taken, the second half of the sermon, and then a closing hymn. That's it. The Lord's Prayer recited (in slightly different translations from time to time) wherever it best fits. The clergy's job is profoundly simple: like Jesus, to take us toward somewhere we Spiritually need to go, and perhaps have never even considered, week after week. If they can not do this, they will keep getting rejected, and frankly, should be.

*

Secondly, the Jews and their disbelief over Jesus as a viable Messiah. While the original Christians were Jewish, a schism evolved between Jews and Christians over Jesus during the 2nd Century, as described, for example, in Justin Martyr's *Dialogue With Trypho*. Paul himself only had a little luck converting Jews to Christians, and during the final phase of the 1st Century (after the Romans destroyed the Temple in 70 C.E.), converts would have been harder to obtain in larger numbers. Scholar Bart Ehrman estimates that there were ca. 10,000 Christians at the end of the 1st Century, still a sizable number. Jews were skeptical of Jesus as a messianic figure from the beginning, having endured previous "false prophets," and could not understand that such a figure could be crucified, the worst form of capital punishment reserved for low-status criminals. This, combined with Jesus' sometimes radical teachings and eventual confrontation with the Temple hierarchy during Passion Week, made Him an unlikely messianic candidate for them. By the end of the 2nd Century, the Jewish-Christian split was firmly in place, and not only because of Paul's relaxation of the Law and circumcision, but because Jews thought he had tried to trample their religion. What men conjured about God had outlasted what God Himself had created, which remains our problem today.

Over the evolving centuries, Jews have largely remained steadfast in their refusal to allow Jesus to be a Messiah. Only in the past forty years, a small number of so-called Messianic Jews have accepted Him as such, much to the consternation of their Jewish brethren. Traditional Jewish objections about Jesus as Messiah involve a variety of concerns: 1) God can not assume human form, which assumes that Jesus was divine; 2) the manner of His death by crucifixion; 3) the third Jewish Temple must be rebuilt; 4) there has been no general resurrection of the dead; 5) all Jews in exile have not yet returned to Israel; 6) there is no global peace; and 7) they offer alternate explanations for Old Testament Scripture which alludes to Jesus' coming as Messiah (e.g., Isaiah 52-53: "the suffering servant"). They lean heavily on Jewish written tradition, including the writings of a 12th Century Jewish sage, Maimonides, who discounts Jesus as a messianic figure.

My problem with such Jewish objections is that any or all of them are born out of only human concerns. By nature, a Messiah comes from God on His own terms, and certainly He does not require our permission to bring forth the Messiah of His choice. Scripture itself was written by humans, even if divinely inspired. None of the 613 Jewish laws pertain to a messianic figure, and the Pharisees and Sadducees disagreed over the topic of resurrection of the dead. Religious tradition, regardless of its source, does not directly equate with obvious divine intervention. I suspect that the Jews are proudly mistaken about Jesus being their Messiah, know they have made a terrible mistake, but are prone not to admit it. I also suspect they know that some other messianic figure is not coming, and so we see a natural drop-off in the percentage of Jews who still "do kosher." Judaism has atrophied from an excess of humanly-dictated teachings which do not allow for the probability that they are wrong about Jesus. I find this sad because there is a long, natural trajectory between Judaism and Christianity which is mutually nourishing, when given the chance. While Jews only number 16-18 million people worldwide, they are our forebearers, and can have much to offer we Christians, if only they would at least read the Gospels after all this time, which tends to be where their "conversion" begins.

*

Lastly, the atheists. While there have always been skeptics about God, historically, most would have allowed for at least the possibility that God exists. In the last century, such skepticism has, for an increasingly larger group, come to be defined by a rather militant insistence that He can not possibly exist, has been disproven by science, and so all "religious fools" are misguidedly ignorant and should accept the obvious: there is no God. This is not the waveringly doubtful agnosticism that many undergo at some point in our spiritual lives, it is a false certainty that borders at times on being menacingly hateful. I spent about six months earlier this year "debating" with atheists on several Facebook groups, basically a waste of time because they have the dual problem of misguided righteousness about "science has explained God" as well as general ignorance about both the Bible as well as how the super-natural could exist. Worst of all, they reject spiritual curiosity as a waste of time, not caring that the rest of us have spent the better part of 4,000 years trying figure out who God is and why He matters.

The seeds of current-day atheism may lie with English philosopher and mathematician, Bertrand Russell, who in 1927 wrote an essay, *Why I Am Not a Christian*. The current generation of atheists (most notably biologist Richard Dawkins and the late Christopher Hitchens) owe much to Russell for at least introducing the strange idea that Jesus never existed. He also can not accept that God has always existed, since "If everything must have a cause, then God must have a cause." This reductionistic argument, which comes from science and not from God, is parroted by Dawkins to develop another strange idea: that there are multiple universes, of which there is currently no proof. Russell thinks that God invented "the Klu-Klux-Klan or the Fascists," apparently not realizing that these are human creations, and God isn't interested in our nastier meet-ups. We hear that "most people believe in God because they have been taught from early infancy to do it," which, while perhaps true, does not account for the variety and richness of our spiritual journeys, occasionally out of atheism and into Christianity. Like Dawkins and comedian Bill Maher, Russell confuses God with religions, as though they are one and the same. He states that religion is based primarily upon fear, which begs the question: fear of what? If I don't believe in God, what is He going to do to me? Likely, nothing. Russell wants to replace God and religion with "a fettering of free intelligence" to relieve our ignorance. He gave up on Christianity at the ripe old age of eighteen, and his father was a disbeliever. Without knowing about Russell's essay, atheists mimic his weak arguments as a way of not having to deal with the super-natural or God's invisibility.

Having this irritating experience of attempting to enlighten often angry male atheists, I came to the conclusion that their perspective is parasitic upon religion and spirituality because they have nothing to offer beyond "what is the proof of your argument" that God exists. Over and over, I heard "what is your evidence" to prove God's existence, a shallow trap because they knew I could not readily produce such evidence. If I spoke of the research on the Shroud of Turin, it was a hoax because of now-faulted 1988 radio-carbon dating fiasco. Atheists basically keep their forefingers in their ears because, if they take them out, doubts about their own position will occur. They also rejected videos of medical miracles by physicians who knew better, not wanting doubt to surface. Atheism is an air-tight thought experiment which allows nothing inside in order to preserve the delusion that God can not exist. C.S. Lewis famously said that atheism is simple, and it is. Always remember: Jesus never existed, because they said so.

*

So, how is Christianity stuck, because of and despite these three disparate "tribes?" It is stuck because these tribes and the general Christian populace are, unlike Jesus, not really pushing the boundaries of the familiar to look at our collective purpose. If the Jews and the atheists cling to a collective NO about God and Jesus, the only consequence is a diminished Christian community in numbers of followers, but no seriously detrimental impact otherwise. They are mildly corrosive, but no worse.

But what are two billion Christians to do with ourselves these days? When I again left the church over five years ago, I personally had given up on the clergy to help me with my Christian journey, as they had nothing serious to offer. I could either do nothing or take on the job of nudging myself forward on my own, which has actually been quite beneficial. I have look at both Judaism and atheism from a distance along with Catholicism, the historical milieu of 1st Century Jesus as well as other interests. Most importantly, I think I have begun to understand how God actually works, and written about this in several essays. Not everyone can or will want to do this work. It is not so much hard as time consuming, but for me, certainly worthwhile. It can be hard to maintain our spiritual curiosity in the face of our daily world as well as God's invisibility. The greatest task is to meld a personal sense of God with what Jesus calls us to do: *to flex our spiritual muscles in the world*. Few people can do both equally well, and I am not yet one of those who can. It is too easy to merely be a contemplative Christian, which has been the Achilles' heel of so many of us. Jesus' brother, James, was at least half-right: faith without works is not dead, but neither is it enough by itself. Despite her idiosyncrasies, I do admire

Mother Teresa's tenacious need to aid the poor. Catholic priests admire their saints while also molesting altar boys. God shakes His head and groans about us each and every day.

I feel God lurking behind me, gesturing to me to keep walking, at least somewhere other than where I already am.

August 2019

WHO WAS AND IS JESUS CHRIST?

After reading British historian Michael Grant's (still available) strong yet concise introductory 1977 treatise on Jesus, it oddly occurred to me that I have not written anything at length about Him. Grant quite rightly describes Jesus as the most influential person who ever lived, so perhaps every Christian (and Messianic Jew) should at least attempt to write down something on His behalf, in terms of how and why He matters to those of us who readily accept His importance. Grant's book is one of a half-dozen or so scholarly books I have read about Jesus, and all of them are differently useful, with their constant caution that we know far too little about Him beyond the Gospels, and yet the swelling popularity of the Christian faith over the subsequent centuries throughout the Roman Empire and beyond can not be denied. Also oddly, no one really talks about what Jesus has been doing in Heaven for nearly two thousand years, other than the Catholic formulary that He "sits on the right hand of the Father," found in the Apostles' Creed. Who was and is Jesus, really, if we try to hold Him in our hands as someone to ponder and receive His inspiration, someone urging us out into the world to better serve the poor, and someone who endured terrorable agony on the Cross in the quasi-voluntary posture of Isaiah's Old Testament "suffering servant" of God? How do we limit our tendency to project our needs and ideas onto Jesus to fill in the holes of our admitted ignorance about Him, knowing that anything we conjure or accept will necessarily and frustratingly be, at most, only half-right?

Jesus' life began, for us but not for Him, with too much opaque history. Was he born, as tradition claims, in Bethlehem, or in Nazareth, as Grant and some other scholars speculate? While it was and is a four-day walk between the two towns, there was also Joseph's obedience to the Roman census decree. Was He born of the still-virginal Mary, as (only) told in Luke's Gospel, and as a descendent of the Davidic line, as told in genealogical fashion (only) in Matthew's Gospel? Was Joseph Jesus' biological or step-father? How many siblings did He have, since the Catholic notion that Jesus was an only child is clearly not accurate? Despite much research and speculation, we still do not know, and likely will never know. As with God, there are (too) many unknowables. The story of Jesus in the Temple preaching at age twelve may or may not be historically accurate, though it takes on added import because there is so little history to work with. Then there is what I call "the long apprenticeship" for some twelve years before Jesus began His ministry around age thirty. Scholars describe Him working as a *tekton*, a laborer of some sort, perhaps in nearby Sepphoris, after learning one or more trades from Joseph. I am inclined to think that Jesus knew how to read (which one scholar doubts), whether gifted this by God or by schooling probably does not matter. He presumably studied the Old Testament (the *Tanakh*) for years, perhaps consulting rabbis as needed. I do not think there was any sense of even quasi-divinity during this period: no healings or miracles. While God talks to Moses almost constantly in the book of Deuteronomy, He does not do so at all regularly in the Gospels with Jesus, so their "conversations" during and after this apprenticeship must have taken on a different sort of style, with mutual understanding to a greater extent. Perhaps Jesus evolved during this apprenticeship as to His eventual mission, if not necessarily its awful outcome. It seems nearly unbelievable that there was no "getting ready" in some fashion during this long period, yet no one ever even speculates about this, except that Jesus "grew in stature and knowledge." Did He keep working during this time, or did His bond with God come to supersede any time for employment, since Jesus had no family to raise? As I do not buy the whole "marriage with kids to Mary Magdalene" hypothesis, the real question is how Jesus spent His free time for twelve years — was He then truly sin-less and what out of this period sustained Him later on with His disciples in dealing with the Jewish religious hierarchy and eventually the Romans?

With this paucity of clarified historical material about Jesus even before His ministry got underway, from the beginning both the Gospel authors and later on the Church attempted to fill in the holes in His story, either through embellishment or dogma. Everyone says and knows this, and yet such conjuring has never ceased and continues to provoke strenuous disagreements, among both scholars and church denominations to this day. What we do not know and probably will never know with any certainty fuels this speculative industry, thus changing the meaning of Gospel from "good news" to "hard and certain truths." I am not inclined to accept that Jesus was forever sin-less, at least not prior to the start of His ministry, since I also do not accept the Trinitarian notion that He is co-equal with God, and therefore perfect. Whatever sins He may have committed, they were milder than my own — that much I do accept. We must acknowledge both our historical ignorance of Jesus' life as well as our very human tendency to fill in its gaps with too much speculation and doctrine as our starting place with Him. There will be no sufficiently reliable evidence or witnesses, no audio or videotape, to persuade nearly anyone of His teachings, His miracles, His crucifixion or resurrection. Atheists love to dwell on this as their principal belief that Jesus either never existed or was no son of God. We all wish it was so simple, but He shines too brightly to be that opaque.

*

Last year, after too many years, I re-read the four Gospels, from a new American translation by Notre Dame's David Benton Hart. Often scholars and sometimes the clergy remind us that each Gospel author was writing to a particular audience in Palestine, but the clergy rarely tells us about the vicissitudes of fact verses embellishment or even fabrication in these works. Two of the four Gospel authors could not have been eyewitnesses, taking stories from Peter and less-so Paul to portray Jesus from description rather than personal experiences. There is also the never-seen "Q" material, upon which the Synoptic Gospels drew as well. Compared to the Old Testament, this story-telling better straddles the fence between the possible and the actual, such that only sometimes was I incredulously saying "Is this really true?" I was more struck by the amount of *plagiaristic* (yes!) repetition in both Matthew and Luke, heavily drawing from Mark's earliest Gospel. Aside from Matthew's genealogy and Luke's birth narrative, Matthew gets less derivative the longer he goes, while Luke gets less interesting later on. I would argue that Matthew and Luke could be trimmed significantly in modern Biblical translations, such is their limited original appeal. Plagiarism, like embellishment and fabrication, has little use in our modern and more literal culture, and renders suspect the larger value of their work. Being a poet and for many years a composer myself, I have no real patience with such "copy cat" material, regardless of whether or not it is culturally sanctioned. Others would likely disagree, and do find these Gospels singularly useful.

With some exceptions then, I gained more from Mark's and John's Gospels than from the two middle-written ones. Mark's Gospel is energetically journalistic to a point, while John's is more meditatively quasi-divinistic. I do not, however, agree that John's Gospel attempts to render Jesus as co-equal to God, as He repeatedly denies such a declaration in favor of His (human) subservience to "Abba, (my) Father." I prefer John's Gospel over the earlier ones, because it has a greater range of events and lengthier discourses from Jesus Himself in the middle portion. It singularly has the Lazarus resurrection, along with Jesus' questioning of Peter about his devotion to Jesus, *after* the latter's resurrection. We even get the specific counting of 153 fish in a net. For me, Mark and John thus serve as the best-known foundations for where to begin concerning our contemplation of Jesus Christ. Other sources, particularly the Roman historian, Josephus, only tell us that He existed, but too little more. There will never be enough factual information about Jesus to satisfy anyone, though we do have the cherished Shroud of Turin (*John 20:1-9*).

*

So what is the plausibly factual picture of the duration and scope of Jesus' ministry in his native Israel in the 1st Century CE? This Jewish healer-teacher-prophet-*Mashiach* and Son of God traveled throughout portions of Israel, with at least several visits to Jerusalem to attend the Jewish festivals, for two to three years (John's Gospel mentions three Passovers), which scholars generally find to be reasonable. After displaying a slightly miraculous tendency at a wedding in Cana, during which He *merely* turned water into wine, Jesus' family and other towns-people turned against Him in Nazareth, and so His itinerant mission began in earnest. Jesus' relationship with John the Baptist (perhaps His cousin) is the subject of some scholarly debate: was Jesus originally a disciple of John's for perhaps several months or even a few years, or did they first met at the River Jordan, when John baptized Jesus to begin His ministry? All four Gospels portray Jesus as an extra-ordinary young man: full of spiritual wisdom, a spell-binding teacher and repeatedly a miraculous healer. He is of little value to us, two thousand years later, if these basic descriptions of Him are not historically true, since other such persons are nearly lost to history. Jesus Christ can not only be the nicest guy we have never met.

About the disciples. Jesus chose twelve young men like Himself, some having been followers of John, to represent the twelve tribes of Israel re-gathered for His spiritual purpose: to up-raise the Jews out of their chronic sense of idolatry and oppression. These disciples were likely not well-educated, perhaps could not read, and spent their time trying to decipher Jesus' words and actions on a daily basis — largely in a state of perpetual confusion, yet also deeply attracted to what He was saying and doing. It remains surprising that none of them abandoned Jesus during His ministry, even long before the end. I have repeatedly read and heard both scholars and the clergy deriding these disciples, but my response to this is *Could you have done any better, knowing the story as you do?* His disciples needed to see Jesus after the resurrection, not just Thomas but all of them, and their own subsequent martyred deaths define their devotion to Him.

The four Gospels tell many stories about Jesus' mission, some fleetingly and others in greater detail. The chronology sometimes gets jumbled, some of the details are slippery, and clearly the authors want to present Him positively. We always have to remember the Gospels are being written to impress others about Him, to the point of, I believe, perhaps sometimes just making things up. Jesus walking on water in a storm while the disciples are stranded in a boat does not seem to have an overarching purpose. Barrabas may well be a fictional character, since there is no historical evidence for a Roman law allowing Pontius Pilate to spare a prisoner at Passover. How can we know what Jesus says to God in Gethsemane or that He agitatedly bled sweat when He was alone? We can only compare our intermittent dis-ease with some details of these stories to the swelling turmoil the disciples feel ongoingly. Any reader of the Gospels has to answer a basic question: does the main thrust of spiritual purpose of Jesus make sense to us, despite the style of story-telling, and what do we do with what we read for ourselves and others? What do we do with this frequent sense of utter astonishment and sometimes fear that Jesus (*Yeshua*) provoked in His Jewish brethren?

All four Gospels spend considerable time on Jesus' arrest, trial, crucifixion, and variably so, His resurrection. Amidst this situation, I do not fault Judas Iscariot as "the worst person who ever lived," as I do not think Jesus actually said this about one of His own disciples. Judas wanted Jesus' mission to be heard by the Sanhedrin, nor do I think he expected to be paid for his efforts. If Judas did hang himself, that is explanation enough. Jesus rather circuitously winds up before Pontius Pilate, who was removed from office by the Romans in 36 C.E. for being excessively brutal, so how does this fact square with his rather lenient posture in the Gospels? Jesus was soon scourged, itself a horrible punishment, before then dragging the cross-beam to Golgotha to be crucified. There are about 120 lash-marks on the body on the Shroud of Turin, and this treatment alone could define Jesus as something other than a mere mortal, since He almost volunteers for this torture. Nearly all of His disciples either denied knowing Him or did not show up for the crucifixion, again not surprising, since by this point they were beyond being perplexed. Several women were brave enough to witness Jesus dying on the cross, as women have always been more votively inclined than we men ever since. After reading a detailed medical description of crucifixion, I fainted for the one and only time in my life, so their bravery admiringly stuns me. "John" (described as Jesus' favorite disciple, not necessarily one of the Twelve) found both the Shroud of Turin and the Sudarium of Oviedo (face-cloth) in the tomb, and so "everything begins" as to who He might *really* be: the end-less speculation, the dogma — yet something "goes divine."

*

As we know, Jesus subsequently appeared not only to His disciples, but also to perhaps many others, after His resurrection. Historians, such as Grant, immediately say that this can not be confirmed factually, which is almost true. If we look at what occurred in the lengthy time that comes (mainly the rest of the 1st Century C.E.), then something originally important had occurred: Paul's conversion, the disciples' martyrdom, and the rather still-inexplicable increase in Christian "membership" after Paul's death in ca. 64 CE as well as the First Jewish Revolt (66-70 CE), which resulted in their second Temple being destroyed by the Romans. Paul had not been significantly successful in converting many Jews to the new Christian faith, largely relying on polytheistic Gentiles looking for "something new." This evolving schism between Christians and Jews would harden by the end of the 2nd Century CE, and remains so to this day. The real question is how this expansion steadily occurred at a rate of 30-40% increase *per decade* until Constantine made Christianity an approved religion in the Roman Empire in the early 4th Century CE, by which time there were more than three million Christians. This expansion and some reasons for its success are described in New Testament scholar Bart Ehrman's newest book, *The Triumph of Christianity* (2018). These include: 1) the steady shrinkage of paganism, partly due to their chronic weariness in having so many gods to worship; 2) the evangelizing mission of Christianity, which was a religiously novel approach; and 3) people saw examples of Christian service to others, which could not be explained away. Most converts to Christianity were initially, like the disciples, poorer and under-educated, but later the wealthy and better-educated began to follow suit. Is there something else that best explains this "triumph of success?"

Unlike we modernly skeptical people, in the 1st Century CE the possibility or likelihood that there was a super-natural plane of existence was readily accepted. There was no real science yet to persuade them otherwise. Somehow those who had witnessed Jesus' resurrection convinced those who had not that this event had actually occurred, and so He was to be worshipped in the company of others who also "believed." The rub is that belief and experience are hardly the same, and once the disciples and others who had originally witnessed Jesus' resurrection had died, how did Christianity continue to spread? Ehrman posits the concept of "going to Hell" as a persuasive factor, but why would this be sufficiently explanatory? That concept is more reflective of the Catholic Church, which slowly organized itself beginning around the 4^{th-5th} Century, with Augustine as a principal inspiration. By then, there were already millions of Christians. There were certainly early Christian martyrs, but that also seems insufficient. The Gospels were not yet organized in book form, and most people were illiterate. Paul's on-going influence after his death is at best unclear. Dogma in the Catholic Church evolved over centuries. In his wonderful book, *The Triumph of Christianity* (2011), sociologist Rodney Stark posits Christian service to the victims of multiple plagues in the Roman Empire during the second and third centuries as a significant influence on pagans to convert, since altruism was considered anathema in their own religious thinking. Perhaps this puts to rest the old "faith vs. works" controversy, from James on to Martin Luther: do Jesus' work, and we shall become popular.

The only thing that may truly explain the "triumphant success" of Christianity's growth from the Roman Empire to Europe would be Jesus' resurrection itself, as no such event, as confirmed by first-hand witnesses, had ever occurred before in the history of humankind. Our acceptance of Jesus basically depends on whether His resurrection makes sense to us — chafing against our scientific orientation, yet harnessed by it nonetheless. He was hardly the only person to be crucified, that being the awful prelude to Easter morning. Crucifixion and resurrection are bound together for Jesus — one without the other is not enough. It is however His resurrection becomes true in each one of us. For many people, this comes from the Bible and from church. For others, there must also be "something else." For me, it is that peculiar photographic cloth, measuring three by fourteen feet, hanging in a chapel in Turin, Italy since 1578, that matters most. An off-color replica hangs in one of my bedrooms. Yet everything we know about Jesus also matters. *Maybe it is only He who truly fingers our souls.*

*

Pope Benedict XVI posited that our Christian faith hangs on the crucifixion and resurrection, since, as Grant points out, Jesus otherwise failed in His mission in Palestine. He was abandoned by nearly everyone at the end, and, had there been no resurrection, He too would likely be merely an historical curiosity as another Jewish "false prophet" who raised their hopes to be released from Roman rule. All the parables and other teachings, all the miracles and the crucifixion were not enough to convince the shakily faithful that He was indeed the *Mashiach*, their Messiah. Grant surmises that Jesus was uncomfortable with all of the labels attached to Him, hence His evasive answers before Pilate when asked: *Who are you?* The question for everyone who could not have witnessed either Jesus' crucifixion or return amongst us, down through all the many centuries, is *what does this mean?* How do we "believe in the unseen," occasionally to the point of martyrdom? *What was the real purpose of Jesus Christ?*

The Catholic Church, through dogmatic teachings in the centuries after Jesus, tried to answer this question with what illiterate people could more easily remember: He died for our sins, as Jesus Himself said, He came to aid the poor and heal the sick as well as showing us how to better treat each other. There is atonement for our sins, there is transubstantiation during the Eucharist, there is the veneration of Mary and a sense of what Heaven might be like. This all can become overly vague symbolism, which slides into churchy platitudes and thus congregational head-scratching. Jesus too easily becomes what we can say about Him in words and phrases that form creeds to be memorized, as though that is enough. Reciting creeds makes us holier only for that moment, which then tends to evaporate too soon. Rather, *we never forget what Jesus Himself said and did.* He worked outdoors a lot as time went on, bypassing the synagogues that hemmed Him in, as with the Sermon on the Mount, not having to worry so much about rain in Palestine. Jesus, before the Christian church fully formed, interests me the most — less than three centuries before the Council of Niacea provoked and never really settled the long parade of incessant bickering about who and what Jesus was and is. It began with the Trinity, and it has never stopped. Jesus could have explained what "Father, Son and Holy Spirit" meant to Him. It would have helped, a lot.

Who was Jesus Christ? He was our tangible, clutchable human linkage to God for a very few years, the kind of radiance that shines beyond Him upon us once we stop to ponder our world. Jesus transcended traditional Judaism by rendering Himself both the embodiment and the sacrifice —not of lambs, but as a man — bringing God into a newly-acute Jewish focus which could not be ignored. After many years in the spiritual wilderness, I now see Him all the time, because I can. As with God, we most commonly come to Him, not the other way around. How many generations of Christians are envious of those first ones who witnessed Jesus outright, to experience that intensity of spiritual surprise, to be slapped awake by the hand of God?

*

As no one ever speculates about Jesus' "long apprenticeship," no one ever speculates about what He has been doing since reaching Heaven, in ca. 30 CE. The strangest part of being a Christian is knowing that He in whom we believe remains unseeable, unless we are granted His visitation, all of our lives. *What does Jesus do in Heaven?* We do not know. It is said that He watches over us, as does God. Does He grant prayerful wishes, or is that God's job? For me, Jesus became swollenly divine as His mission continued, and became fully divine at the moment of His resurrection. Do we become divine when we die? We assume so. I pray to God rather than to Jesus, because I can not articulate His own particular purpose in Heaven, that He still mainly "works for God." Thus, Jesus is always spoken of as a past living figure, that, ironically, His resurrection leaves us without a seeable man to learn from and be inspired by to live our lives. We are told that it had to be this way, which is true. We have to come to Him, to partake of His body and blood (in what one rabbi crudely calls "ritualistic cannibalism"), introject or absorb Him as best we can, and do so on a daily basis for the rest of our lives. Hopefully, it never stops. Every day, He hangs on my bedroom wall, and I look at Him — that is the best church. The long, longest time since He died shrinks down to nothing as I find Him yet again. God said it had to be this way. Finally, there is no real absence from Him. *Amen.*

January 2020

WHY JESUS' CRUCIFIXION SICKENS US

Each year, in Christian churches during Passion Week, the subject of Jesus' crucifixion is described in elusive terms, but rarely in much detail. Often, there is merely the statement: "Jesus was crucified," with relevant Scripture passages cited, which itself tells this part of the story rather briefly, again, with sparser details. Maundy Thursday and Good Friday involve vaguer recollections of His suffering, Scripture lessons and melancholic hymns. All of this is obviously necessary and appropriate, but, as I wrote in a previous essay about God's invisibility, such merely allusive descriptions neither do the horrendous suffering of Jesus any real justice, nor help us to internalize why His crucifixion is so central to our understanding of Jesus' purpose on earth. His crucifixion is rarely mentioned in churches at any other time of the year, other than in passing. This central, pivotal event, without which our faith would not have blossomed, receives little attention and less clarification by either theologians or the clergy, hence is revered by the rest of us mostly for those who wear crosses around our necks. Those who have seen the Shroud of Turin, either in person or through photographs, have a better sense of Jesus' suffering, yet even this is a photograph after the fact. Church attendance at either Maundy Thursday or Good Friday services tend to pale in comparison with those of Easter Sunday for a reason: there is no sadness, there is no suffering and we do not feel nauseous. As Dr. Frederick Zugibe, a forensic pathologist, wrote his book summarizing many years of relevant medical research, *The Crucifixion of Jesus* (2005): "It is profoundly important that the full impact of Jesus' agony in Gethsemane and on the Cross is not generally recognized among Christians." This is because we do not know, and do not want to know, since it dredges up the old question: *Why did God let Him suffer so?*

Gospel accounts that are specifically relevant to crucifixion, contain bits of detail, but move steadily elsewhere toward Jesus' resurrection.

Luke's Gospel mentions that Jesus sweat blood (*hematidrosis*) in Gethsemane while asking God to be released from crucifixion, but little else in detail afterward. The other three Gospels mention Jesus being scourged by Roman soldiers, the crown of thorns, being battered by a rod on the head, Jesus carrying His cross to Golgotha and later being pierced in the side with a lance to determine if He was dead. Mocking and spitting, earthquakes and the tearing of Temple veil add dramatic touches, but that is about it. Crucifixion, being such a common occurrence in the Roman world, was familiar to everyone, and so did not need any literary elaboration. Rather it is we who find it hard to conjure this really at all, since *crucifixion is unimaginable*. In Mel Gibson's grisly portrayal, *The Passion of the Christ (*2004*)*, even the flogging goes on for seemingly forever as a prelude to Jesus' crucifixion, and as such is an emotional overload for nearly anyone. Dr. Zugibe complains about the details of how Gibson portrays the crucifixion, but we are drained nonetheless. This film is the only source I know of that even comes close to the real thing, aside from detailed medical descriptions, such as in Lee Strobel's *The Case For Christ* (1998), which provoked me to faint many years ago.

*

I will draw from Dr. Zugibe's quite detailed medical description of the relevant Gospel accounts of Jesus' crucifixion to amplify my premise as to its "distasteful" qualities. As mentioned, He sweat blood in Gethsemane, which reflects numerous other cases of hematidrosis arising from great acute anxiety, not only while fearing crucifixion, but also from, for example, a sailor being caught in an intense storm or a child frightened by a gas explosion. In addition to sweating blood, Jesus would likely have felt weak, dehydrated and psychologically morose. He was later scourged with a *flagrum*, a whip-like instrument with leather straps with small metal or bony balls, which would dig into the victim's flesh with repeated lashings. Roman soldiers could strike the victim many times, often disregarding the Jewish custom of no more than 39 lashes. Jesus would have been (largely) naked and shackled by the wrists to a post. His breathing from the blows would have become labored, with eventual pain in his back muscles and ribs. Tremors, vomiting and seizures may well also have occurred, which in victims tended to produce aspects of shock. The crown of thorns applied by the Roman soldiers was not the simple circular creation often portrayed in paintings or films — it more resembled a helmet or cap, with long thorns which dug into His scalp, producing extensive bleeding. As the scalp has many blood vessels, this would be almost unbearably painful. Jesus then carried the *patibulum*, or cross-beam (which weighed ca. 60 lbs.), to Golgotha for perhaps as long as a half-mile, stumbling repeatedly along the way, with no means to break His fall. As the Roman soldiers did not want victims to die on the way to crucifixion, this may be why Simon of Cyrene was enlisted to help Jesus. He would be dehydrated, dizzy and short of breath, as at least one of His lungs may well have collapsed. Catholics rightly memorialize this terrorable journey with their Stations of the Cross in old Jerusalem as well as in all their parishes.

Crucifixion had been used as a persuasive punishment for various crimes since perhaps as early as the Sixth century BCE by various cultures, though it is best known for its pervasive usage by the Romans from the Third century BCE. Only one physical example of crucifixion as ever been found, a heel bone with a nail through it, despite tens of thousands of crucifixions. Iron nails were repeatedly used, as with Jesus, although other victims were also tied to their crosses with ropes. When nails were used to pierce the hands and feet, this created severe pain called *causalgia*, which does not respond even to morphine. After His lengthy walk to Golgotha, Jesus was thrust to the ground and hoisted upon the cross, which itself was quite painful. He likely screamed out in agony before and after his wrists were nailed, which pinched or severed the medial nerve in His hand, provoking the causalgia. Plantar nerves in His feet would be similarly painful when pierced. Dr. Zugibe suspects each foot was nailed separated out of convenience to the soldiers. Jesus' heart would have beaten rapidly, with profuse sweating and blood loss, inducing more shock. His body weight against the nails in His hands and feet would have been unbearable. Nearly all scholars and physicians agree that Jesus was crucified for about six hours, an unusually short time for such a punishment, as many victims remained alive on crosses for days or even a week. Dr. Zugibe determined the cause of Jesus' death to be: "Cardiac and respiratory arrest, due to hypovolemic and traumatic shock." In essence, Jesus began dying from the scourging onward, having had nothing to eat or drink since the Last Supper.

Dr. Zugibe discounts the commonly-cited cause of death as primarily respiratory distress from the position of His body upon the cross, and he also dismisses the multitude of versions of what is known as "the Swoon Theory": that Jesus somehow survived the crucifixion, even if He died later. It is clear that only physicians can fully understand the intricacies of medical functioning in relation to how the body is repeatedly compromised during crucifixion. I find this approach helpful, if a little nauseating. It does take us back to the old question, however: *Why did God let Jesus suffer so?*

*

A different version of the same question is: *why did Jesus have to die by crucifixion*, and not some other, less gruesome method, if He had to be killed at all? Let us look at Passion Week first. Prior to that time, He was not in any serious trouble with the Roman authorities, though He had aroused both the curiosity and wrath of His fellow Jewish Temple figures, which swelled in earnest after the raising of Lazarus in the days before Jesus arrived in Jerusalem for the last time. His triumphant entry on a donkey was soon eclipsed by His own provocation at the money changers' tables, challenging the norms of the Temple, and thus courting retaliation. It is this action, and not so much Judas Iscariot's betrayal of Jesus, that is the primary provocation eventually leading to His crucifixion. *Jesus is trying to get Himself killed by His own people,* under the auspices of the Romans. I wrote an earlier essay on this subject, and accept that Jesus was clearly doing God's will in this regard. He knew He would be killed, likely by crucifixion, accepting the necessity of this outcome until His hematidrosis at Gethsemane.

It is mildly important to note that I do not believe in the Trinity. In this context, that means Jesus' provocation at the Temple, with His clear intent to get arrested, taken under Jewish trial and Roman crucifixion, was made by a young human man, and not by Himself as God. He is "betting" on being resurrected afterward, yet His hematidrosis at Gethsemane and crying out the opening lines of Psalm 22 on the cross do not sound like a god, since gods don't suffer terrorably and die. I really do not like the old church notion of Jesus' "victory over death" — there is no such "victory," as He has to die to get resurrected — as we have seen, a very painful death. It is this death which allows both the Shroud of Turin to be created in the tomb as well as for His resurrection to occur, and clearly reveal the existence of God, really for the first time. It is Mary Magdalene who witnessed Jesus suffering on the cross after His disciples had scattered, and, in John's Gospel, it is she who later tells them that He has risen. It is she who witnesses His suffering and is also visited by the resurrected Jesus to confirm His transcendence.

It is this combination, the terrorable crucifixion and the radiant resurrection, that serves as the foundation of our Christian faith. Everything that comes later is merely theology and religion, in comparison. To answer the above question: *It had to be this way*.

May 2020

WHAT IS SPIRITUAL INTROJECTION?

During a lengthy period of reading, listening to historical material about early Christianity on DVDs as well as my own thinking, I consider it seems that hardly anyone has ever clearly described or explained how we are to become spiritualized human beings. The Bible tends to describe this in examples of sudden transformation, such as through the miracles of Jesus. For most of us, however, the so-called "spiritual journey" tends to evolve more slowly and unsteadily, often taking years or even decades to mature into anything resembling a personal consistency between faith and action, introspection and charity or reconciling the Natural world with the divine realm of altered space and time, as described by those who have (usually unluckily) visited Heaven during near-death experiences. The Church, whether Catholic or Protestant (or Jewish, for that matter), tends to rely mostly on doctrines and worship services for this purpose, along with the occasionally inspired sermon. Few in the Church ever really ask: how do we help to make our parishioners more spiritual, less egocentric and capable of finding God in our lives during the other six days of the week?

I have become interested in the (pre-Catholic) history of early Christianity because I want to try to understand "what went wrong" after Jesus and Paul died, after the Gospels were written, when we no longer had any of "the originals" left to tell us about what actually happened during Jesus' ministry. My bias about the Gospels is that they are stories formed to tell us about Jesus to show the range of His work on earth, but they can feel static, and it is too easy to reduce the Gospels to something akin to a textbook to be endlessly recited and studied over our lifetimes. They feel more like photographs than moving pictures, and I sense that "the real story" of Jesus was actually different and perhaps even more interesting than what we can only read of Him. What would the moment-to-moment, day-to-day life of His disciples have been like, since we barely hear from most of them in the Gospels? It is clear that they struggled to understand Jesus, particularly His notion of "the Kingdom of God," how they were to continue His work after His resurrection, and what was their evolving sense of God's divine realm? If we assume that most of the disciples were largely illiterate, they could not even read the Old Testament (*Tanakh*), and so knew of their Judaism primarily through indoctrination from family and their synagogues. Jesus tried to pull them out of "what had always been," though He was only partially successful until the disciples could witness His resurrection.

Judaism itself has been described as a "book religion," though God is not a book, and He never had to write anything. I do not believe in the notion of Biblical inerrancy, so I don't think we can absorb Him merely by reading endlessly. Jewish rituals and festivals, the 613 laws, circumcision and purification, the dietary laws and insular culture have served to form a sort of Jewish religious social psychology that said this is how we find God: through Scripture study, remaining obedient to the Law and keeping to ourselves. But the Old Testament frequently returns to Jewish disobedience toward God, including idolatry and wanton sinfulness. Multiple prophets railed against this, often to no avail. Many Jews today do not keep kosher laws, perhaps out of cultural weariness. Aspects of Judaism, particularly the prohibition on eating pork and shellfish along with circumcision, strike me as pagan, and not likely to lead to a genuine, fully-formed spiritual life. Judaism is too dependent on texts, rituals and history to ignite a broad-based, muscular spirituality that is not merely a reflection of their historical religious culture. Hence Jesus, whom they generally reject as a Messianic figure. Some early Christian writers, such as Justin Martyr, mocked the Jews' religious preoccupations by calling them "superstitious." What did God want the disciples of Jesus to do with His more radical message of nudging Judaism to nearly its breaking-point, which wound up getting most of them martyred?

The Catholic church replaces the 613 laws, circumcision and the dietary restrictions with its own more conceptual doctrines, honoring of Mary and their saints with a strong dose of discouraging sin through regular church attendance. I recently watched a video of a Latin Mass, which is highly prized by many in the Catholic church, and found it curious but rather hollow. It is highly choreographed for the clergy, interesting to watch (once in a while), but ultimately does not really qualify as a deeply spiritual experience for me. It is clear that there is great admiration for Judaism by Catholics, who see a kinship of rituals and immoral prohibitions indoctrinated through catechism in children. Like Judaism, Catholicism relies upon its history of practices more than any alembical challenges toward a personal spirituality. Certainly, there is a lengthy history of Catholic writers who looked deeply into Christian spirituality, but not in terms of any integration of individual psychology and spiritual transcendence that can be put into practice, with the possible exception of Mother Teresa. I am likely being unfair to both religions, but, from the outside, this is how they strike me.

Protestantism, as it has evolved, has lost focus and become too bland. It means too many things to different people, and the denominational strife over homosexuality in recent years highlights its inertia and intolerance. Seven years ago, I left the Presbyterian church because it has never really had much to offer me, it was what I was born into as a child. My problem was that I never had a satisfying church home, and so gave up trying to find one. God and Jesus, in contrast to the church, have always been more interesting. How do we become genuinely spiritual without the aid of non-viable churches?

*

It was in the 2nd Century CE that the early Christians began to try to make sense of what Jesus was all about. Their handicap was that, once the last of the Apostles and their followers died, there were no living brethren from whom to extract what made Jesus uniquely special in religious history. Although the Gospels were circulating and initial attempts at forming a New Testament canon were being made, what began to take too much precedence was theology, and not just the Trinity. Early attempts at theological discourse can be seen in the Apostolic Fathers during the first half of the 2nd Century as the early, pre-Catholic church settled into its rhythm of establishing a permanent presence in religious society. Jesus could now only be conjured and contemplated, but never again could He be directly witnessed, and this loss has haunted Christianity ever since. In an earlier essay, I described how God's invisibility led to the development of theology in all religions, as it serves as the primary vexing point for how we are to understand Him. Theology began to replace experiences as the primary route to spiritual discipline and practice, salvation and redemption. One of the worst debates was over faith versus works, which began with Jesus' brother, James, and languished on until Martin Luther, who hardly resolved the matter, at least to my satisfaction. Theology is complex but easier than trying to harness the meaning of having witnessed Jesus, as had the disciples, who wound up writing so little compared to the many, many theologians who would follow them, until the present day. Theology is too much akin to philosophy: both can be purposeful, but both can too easily miss the mark. Theology's dominance in these early centuries became clotted enough for Constantine, as a newly-converted Christian, to gather the Council of Nicaea in 325 CE to try to settle a particular theological dispute, again with only partial success. Theology can be like wet soap in our hands: grasping it too tightly often leads to its slipping onto the shower floor.

We are thus caught in a permanent bind regarding Jesus and His disciples: we can read about them every day and year, we can contemplate them theologically, all the while too largely denied any certain historical clarity as to what they actually said and did on a daily basis. The Gospels are at best a storied approximation of what happened, a decent set of photographs but not a movie, certainly not videotape, and thus as frustrating as they certainly are "better than nothing." We are never sure what is fact, what is embellishment and what is outright fabrication — yet this is our best source about Jesus and His disciples. No wonder people become discouraged. My own answer to this frustration (as I am studying John's Gospel at the moment, with the aid of priestly and scholarly guides) is to accept this situation as part of the larger set of unknowables: what does God look like, how was the universe actually created, and will there really be a Second Coming. Rather, I would like to attempt to take what we conjure and know to go somewhere else: toward a better sort of spiritual functioning than was described by more than a few Catholic sages over the centuries. We simply need something more, and perhaps something else.

Since none of us has divine abilities to affect others' health or any direct conversations with God, what does it really mean to become an "imitator of Christ?"

*

Introjection is a concept introduced by Sigmund Freud to describe how we are affected by the persistent influences of others, particularly our parents. Introjection illustrates how such influence becomes notable or even dominant in our own behavior. It is being influenced enough to enact an influence at least indirectly to reflect that influence. Although Freud talked about introjection mostly in interpersonal and especially familial terms, it can be seen in other ways. We all introject basic driving rules such as speed limits, stop signs and traffic signals. In a democracy, we vote for candidates who will hopefully reflect our political interests, since democracy is only a concept until it is enacted. Freud thought that parental influences served as the principal introjected material for children, whether positive or not. Children of alcoholics are a clear example of problematic introjection related to witnessing abusive parental drinking, often accompanied by lying and denial, auto accidents and impaired family functioning. This introjection can then be reflected in children's school functioning and life plans, choice of romantic partners and overall happiness.

Introjection becomes "what we carry around inside us" for even decades, which affects how we function as adults. People, whether they realize it or not, often go to psychotherapy to correctively deal with negative introjections. Freud saw this repeatedly with female patients in particular, who intuitively knew of this and would describe it in detail, most common in regard to their poor self-esteem. Introjection, whether for better or worse, is a naturally cumulative process which often leaves an indelible mark on people, sometimes for a lifetime.

Jesus' disciples strived to introject His teachings, miracles and ways of relating to their fellow Jews, not by reading but by witnessing His ministry on a daily basis. He chose them because of sensing some sustainable introjective potential in these twelve men, who could later carry on His work on their own. The Gospels at times reflect His disciples' struggle with introjecting Jesus' words and actions, particularly their reflexive confusion over His miracles. In John's Gospel, they are often confused by or misinterpret what Jesus tells them, and so He corrects them. Jesus offers His disciples a combined maternal and paternal positive introjection to further their own spiritual independence to do God's work in the future after His resurrection and ascension. The eventual success of their introjection is seen in the likely martyrdom of at least some or most of the disciples. Jesus is gifting them something they could never receive otherwise: a direct linkage to God, unobtainable through only reading the *Tanakh* or obeying the Jewish Law. Such introjection would slowly and then more steadily ripple further over the next several centuries to propel Christianity into becoming the dominant religion in the Roman Empire. Introjection is a psychological process which can serve as the foundation for our own evolving spirituality, with God and Jesus leading the way.

While it is admirably necessary to indoctrinate children who attend church with the basic tenets of the Christian faith, this alone will generally prove insufficient to establish any deeper introjected spirituality by itself, beyond a simpler charitable orientation. Even the complex rituals of Judaism are specific to its religious practices, and do not necessarily translate into anything to be used outside the synagogue or home, although Jews will likely disagree. Religion by itself, regardless of type, mainly orients us toward the divine realm and a charitably giving interpersonal stance to the world. But anyone can easily be completely disinterested in God, Jesus, Mohammed or Buddha. Rather, it is how any of these figures become spiritually vital that is of interest here. Religion and spirituality nests itself within our already established introjections by the time we are late teenagers or adults. Young people who attend evangelical churches, sometimes describing themselves as "on fire for God," have introjected an at least rudimentary spirituality to serve others in some fashion, if mainly by spreading the good news of the Gospels. What has come to interest me as a starting place is when people take a suddenly strong interest in reading the Bible because of its distinct descriptions of how God affects His people in a certain place and period of time: namely Jews between ca. 1,500 BC and 90 CE, and what relevance this has for us in now the 21st Century. Book religions must become introjected and not merely discussed and memorized to be of real spiritual value. So how does that happen to some individuals, but so few of us collectively?

Spiritual introjections are both different from and more allusive than what Freud espoused, because, unlike having stop signs or parents to see on a daily basis, God is always invisible, and for us, Jesus is always only readable, or more beneficially to me, viewable in films. The basis for a fuller-voiced Christian faith has to deal with He who is unseeable who gifts us His Son, who is for us also unseeable. Mother Teresa said she heard Jesus talking to her on a train as a young nun, and this is what provoked her to begin her charity work — yet she did not claim to see Him. What can we more easily introject from the Gospel stories about Jesus as a starting place? I would say it is His being a medium for the divine realm, since without both His miracles and resurrection no one would consider Him memorably special. Miracles drew the crowds and His resurrection allowed for the spreading of the faith after His ascension. No other person in the history of the world claimed to be resurrected and then appeared to people on earth afterward. Jews struggle to accept Jesus as their Messiah because crucifixion and resurrection were and are not part of the messianic story of their future. Beyond the parables and other teachings, the miracles and even His Transfiguration, what can be introjected most readily from the Gospels is Jesus serving as an intermediary between God and ourselves, which no other person has ever done. We introject His spiritual uniqueness first, that has to be of interest or nothing else happens. Atheists can not accept the existence of the divine realm because of their materialistically scientific orientation, and so become incapable of spiritual introjection. We Christians instead accept and gravitate toward the divine realm because God lives there, and our bias is that He created the universe nearly 14 billion years ago, probably through the Big Bang. The Natural world is all we see of God, that it belongs first to Him. That is why pantheism is so attractive, because God infuses Himself into our living visible world, which is where our spiritual introjection also begins and daily sustains itself.

If the Gospels render Jesus familiar to us and God is reflected in Nature, how then do we evolve toward what is called "faith in action?" Endlessly reading the Bible as a kind of perennial textbook to be swallowed whole usually does not, by itself, turn us into "imitators of Christ." Jesus never told His disciples *Just read Scripture, just obey the Law*. He prodded them to go out into the world, first by twos and later in the Great Commission. Jesus gave no theological lectures or rehashed the finer points of the Torah. His efforts were for the disciples to introject all that they had heard and witnessed from Jesus to *go and do* for others. But this is how our spiritual introjections flounder: we study the Bible and read related books, go to Bible studies, maybe participate in occasional service projects or even try out mission trips, as some churches do emphasize service work. How does all of this settle and meld into spiritual discipline and service? How far can we nudge ourselves toward gaining faith in action? Why do a relative few succeed in this effort, while many of us plod along and only favorably pretend to be functional Christians?

I answer this question with two more psychological terms: the familiar term *narcissism,* and a less-known word *resistance.* Simply put, narcissism denotes our variably intense self-centeredness which impedes our ability to care for and serve others. Narcissism also describes the limits of our abilities to understand what others are telling us. The disciple Peter sometimes blurts out responses to Jesus which reflect his understandably human perspective, which Jesus then has to correct. When Peter offers to die for Jesus, he is instead told he will deny knowing Jesus several times by the next morning. Such denial is, of course, self-serving in a time of great distress and uncertainty, with Peter correctly fearing that Jesus is about to die. Resistance is what it sounds like — an impaired desire to fraternize and aid unknown others, whether out of disinterest or fear of the unknown. We are often reluctant to help others out of "not wanting to get involved." Narcissism stokes resistance, which results in spiritual inertia. I would say many Christians regularly experience such spiritual inertia, because we are not being pushed by others to grow and help, or resist such prodding. Our Christianity becomes easy and safe. It is what we do on Sundays, and the rest of the week "live our normal lives." One of the Apostolic Fathers, Ignatius of Antioch, was seized by an intense desire for martyrdom, such was his zeal for Jesus, and this eventually occurred. He had been relieved of his narcissism and resistance toward God and Jesus, even though he never met Them. Some Christians are like this: like Ignatius, like Mother Teresa, like Dietrich Bonhoeffer, who was executed during World War II for his faith. Such people are rare, and I am not one of them. I have never been visited by the Holy Spirit, and transformed into a disciple who fully trusts in God as to my life and fate. What are people like me and many other Christians to do about our too-shallow faith to try to live out Jesus' conviction: *go and do*?

My answer so far is to both continue to circle around Jesus' basic stance of serving others when and where possible (akin to the old cliché about the moth and the flame) as well as search out some service activity to pursue on a longer-term basis, since I am retired. My introjection of God and Jesus seems to need some external push at this point to guide me deeper into any real spiritual service. I will continue studying and thinking, as always, since that has helped a lot since I left the church. Other people who have settled into service activities could also provide some guidance.

I close with the last lines of my new poem referencing this material:

                    You will say
it is not the creeds or minded doctrines,
not scratchy catechism or even sacraments
on chaster Sundays,
                    but what gets best
-ly swallowed to walk us farther unto You,

our never-see-able phantasm of Creation
looming behind us to watch & daily wait
          to reveal Your divine surprises,
ineffably unspoken yet peculiarly true,
grains of the divine feasting our tongues.

October 2020

BETTER LATE THAN EVEN LATER
(In praise of Jesus' Disciples)

(Simon) Peter (*Cephas*)	Philip	Nathanael
Andrew	Matthew	Jude (Thaddeus)
James	Thomas	James (Alphaeus)
John	Judas Iscariot	Simon (the Zealot)

Who were the twelve disciples that Jesus chose to begin and fulfill His mission throughout Galilee and eventually Jerusalem? What were these men like and how did they attempt to understand Him, particularly His seemingly divine nature? Why did they ultimately deny, betray and abandon Jesus before His crucifixion and struggle to make sense of His resurrection? How were His disciples both a reflection of the Jewish religious elite as well as our own difficulty in ascertaining the nature of the divine?

In truth, beyond occasional statements by some of these disciples and glimpses of their dealings with Jesus in the four Gospels, we know very little about them. Four of them were fishermen and one a tax collector, but the others' occupations are unclear. We presume most or all of them were not well educated, nor do we know how intelligent they were, at least in spiritual matters. Peter and Nathanael declared Jesus to be the Jewish Messiah (*Mashiach*), though Thomas remained skeptical until after His resurrection in an understandable need for physical proof. Philip, like Moses, asked Jesus to be shown at least God's face, yet John seemed to understand what he was holding in finding (what we call) the Shroud of Turin and the Sudarium of Oviedo in the tomb. Many of these disciples never said anything in the Gospels, and so we know them only by their scattering in the face of collapsing faith after

Jesus was arrested. We only know that all of them witnessed the supernatural repeatedly, but like us, could not easily accept its meaning and purpose. These disciples have too often been disparaged by both the clergy and scholars alike for failing to fully understand Jesus as "the face of God on earth," with one pastor calling them "buffoonish," which strikes me as foolishly arrogant, as though we ourselves have done so much better than those who lived with and survived Jesus. They lived the life of Jesus one day at a time, while we have always known "the rest of the story." We can only be envious of their daily experiences and struggles to even tell each other who Jesus was. Why did they hang around until "after the end?"

*

As has been speculated by scholars, it seems likely that some or most of the disciples had an ongoing familiarity with Jesus beforehand. A few had been involved with John the Baptist, as had Jesus Himself for at least a short while. Presumably Jesus saw a spiritual inclination in all of these men, despite their lack of formal religious training. He knew them to be actively involved in their synagogues, and that they were not religiously disinterested or hostile to His ministry. Whether the disciples actually gave up living with their own families so easily we can not know, since we are reading interpretive stories rather than having any first-hand corroboration. We can know that these men wanted something more than to only be fishermen. They wanted to find God, and Jesus, unlike other false prophets, did not seem deceptive, manipulative or merely fanciful. He was genuine, and they somehow knew this. It is not clear that Jesus performed any miracles to sway their involvement and allegiance, rather it was a sort of intrinsic trust that could be reciprocated and sometimes challenged by Jesus. We do not know how long it took to gather the twelve disciples, whether there were others who were deemed unsuitable, or yet others who "tried Jesus out" and left Him behind. Church tradition describes martyrdom for all but John, though again, there is no historical path to be sure. We do feel certain these disciples largely went their separate ways to further Jesus' work, even amongst the Gentiles.

His disciples agreed to follow Jesus, probably with some mixture of curiosity, uncertainty and a bit of conviction that they had, after some 1,800 years, "found their man." They began with a hunger to know that God exists, that He could be influential in a world where slavery and persecution occur, that idolatry was a too-poor substitute for a viable spiritual Father, and that the Jews in particular had not been forgotten, despite being chosen by God. Jesus seemed like "the right guy," the One sent by God in human form to render His likeness visible to we who can not so easily sight Heaven on our own. What then comes is both the beginning of their spiritual journeys as well as the confusion that will forever mark these disciples as those guys who "dropped the ball," who "ran away at crunch time," and whose faith frayed and withered once events during the Passion quickly out-ran their simpler sense of how God and men work. We are all told to believe that the disciples failed both Jesus and ourselves, that is how the story unfolds on what is strangely called "Good Friday." All of their recurring doubts gelled into the need to be relieved of what no longer made enough sense, yet they could not go so far away. They had to linger to see if anything could become of Jesus' death, or had they also been duped like so many others, false prophets and all?

*

There are so many unknowables in this Jewish and Christian faith. What does God look like, and will we see Him in Heaven? How are any of us to understand the divine realm, even when we witness a miracle ourselves? Was the tomb filled with radiation, as some physicists think, when Jesus was resurrected? Another unknowable is how the disciples talked to and about Jesus amongst themselves on a daily basis. Did they have ongoing conversations about what He said and did, or was confusion the only common emotional language? We know that Jesus had to recurringly explain Himself in clarifying terms for their benefit, and that He sometimes became exasperated in having to do so. I don't think we should presume that there was a predictable level of spiritual understanding about Jesus that any or all of these disciples had that allowed them to be certain of anything beyond the basics of His mission, and that this led to a chronic sense of inferiority and even fear at times, hence the use of "terrified" in describing their reactions to Jesus on occasion. How could Peter expect to walk on water as a mere mortal, since none of us would? Particularly in John's Gospel, Jesus often spoke in a symbolically ambiguous manner, which confused both His disciples as well as the interrogating Pharisees. They were constantly working to make better sense of what He said and did, that the Old Testament (*Tanakh)* (which He presumes they had read more than once) was not enough help, and so they too-often floundered at the level of keeping up with what Jesus meant and wanted from them. They were the students who needed tutoring, but for whom the only tutor was the Master who confused them. There must have been days when one or more of the disciples wanted to quit and go home, go back to their families and lives that could more easily prosper and make sense. I do think Jesus asked too much of His disciples too often, and they retaliated on Good Friday. How could they play hooky with God's Son?

*

Since, as I write, we are again in the midst of Lent, let us blend our own questions, doubts and devotion to Jesus with that of His disciples. Jesus' ministry apparently lasted either one year (the Synoptics) or for at least three Passovers (John's Gospel), and it was for this length of time that the disciples walked, thought and acted in accordance with both their desire to do Jesus' work as well as to soothe the weariness of their own preoccupations about how to render Him sensible to themselves. I don't think they ever did so well enough, since Jesus kept pecking at their heads about the Kingdom of God, about mercy and forgiveness, about social status and the wealth of the divine in the lives of the poor and unfortunate, and, eventually, that too soon, He would have to die. What were they to do with a dead *Mashiach*? Are any of us "buffoonish" when we are told someone we love is going to die? As in any enterprise where things do not always run sensibly or smoothly, the disciples' doubts festered and firmed into the beginnings of a rejection posture: why all of this time and work for seemingly nothing? The urge to bail on Jesus would become acute, like a party that suddenly goes sour. At Gethsemane, the "inner circle" of Peter, James and John (who had become "terrified" upon witnessing the spectacle of the Transfiguration), repeatedly went to sleep as do children who have heard and seen enough. Peter denied Jesus because this "lost cause" meant that he himself had wasted so much time not catching fish to feed his family. Why were there exactly 153 fish (a sort of inexplicable perfect number) on the beach at the end of John's Gospel? Jesus in effect says that He could catch more fish in less time than spiritually wayward Peter did in the usual fashion, sarcastically so. Three times of "Do you love me?" was a sort of communal humiliation for Peter's denial and abandonment of Jesus. Why is this scene never discussed in church? It is not something that God Himself would do, and it colors Jesus to be vindictively human.

Our witnessing a miracle provokes a particular and peculiar psychology in its wake, and the disciples experienced multiple miracles over a span of time, leaving them startled yet confirmed that Jesus must surely be no false prophet. Peter, James and John saw Jairus' daughter raised, witnessed the Transfiguration, and yet had to abandon Jesus because Judaism did not allow for a crucified *Mashiach*. As the Beatles once sang, it was "All Too Much." Jesus stretched and stretched His disciples akin to human taffy and expected them to want to stay awake for the last act because, well, they deserved a sort of happy ending for their efforts. But they couldn't, it was all too much, being spiritually jerked around for how many months away from home, these younger men in love with their women. But they could not go home, Jesus nagged at their love for Him, their devotion to His ministry, so none of them could yet quite give up on Him, seemingly dead forever. Holy Saturday was their awful purgatory for the living followers left behind. It is not as bad as women who can not give up on their adulterous or abusive husbands, but the Passion was horrendous for these exhausted disciples nonetheless. They could only sleep at the wrong time and grieve for He who had abandoned *them*. In a strange twist, the disciples, along with the Pharisees and Sadducees, melded together in a sort of "circle of disbelief" around Jesus, wondering who He really was — all of them Jews, asking *What do we do with and about this guy, who walks His own path, surely Jewish but what else?*

I praise these disciples — no "buffoons" but surely brave beyond our own willingness to walk with Him day after day, not conscripted into some holy army, but rather privileged to bear witness to a Godly emptiness in the tomb, making their martyrdom necessary unto a God who had granted them the realm of the miraculous again and again, human men gifted to drink at the well of the inviolable.

13 March 2021

ONCE GOD SENDS US ELSEWHERE
(Musing about miracles)

In several previous essays, I examined the subjects of God's invisibility as well as the surprising effect of miracles on both Jesus' disciples in particular and the Jews generally. Of the many descriptions of miracles in this 1st Century context, too few highlight well enough this startling sense of bewilderment that was experienced by everyone involved as something quite beyond normal everyday life, and hence its effects were varied yet profound. Only in a few films about Jesus can this be clearly seen. In this essay, I want to shed greater light on the linkages between God's perpetual invisibility, the reactions to Jesus' miracles and how this plays out in both His ministry as well as His eventual crucifixion and resurrection: a sort of psychology of miracles.

We take God's invisibility for granted, to our detriment. His invisibility is the foundation for the best and worst theologies in any and all religions, whether simple or complex, and no matter how many gods are involved, since Jews and Christians accept only one God, while the ancient Egyptians, for example, believed in perhaps a thousand gods. Everything about either Judaism or Christianity stems from God's invisibility: from Moses asking to see God's face to the Jews' 613 religious and dietary laws to the Christian Trinity to the Shroud of Turin. Millions of people revere a cloth created in a perhaps radioactive instant by the first-ever divine photographer, not only because we can finally see Jesus for the first time since ca. 30 CE., but because we can also surmise the divine power of His Father. He whom we shall likely never see (even if we get to Heaven) affects everything about our religious ideas and practices, which often renders them too unnecessarily human. It is always *"this is what we think God is like."* At best, only two of the four Gospel writers reported any eye-witness experiences with Jesus, perhaps John more so than Matthew. God's invisibility affects theology, but, more importantly, it affects how the Jews (and ourselves) experience and interpret miracles, since by nature they fall outside the realm of religious concepts and practices, and indeed, everything else we know. They shake our very spiritual earth, what we thought we know with certainty, our very being. Hence, *no more idols.*

*

Idols do not have any innate capacity to provoke miracles. The Israelites used idols, such as *Baal*, to render God (more) visible as some likeness that allowed Him to "live in their homes." Moses became angry because his fellow Jews could not stand to have "nothing to look at" day after day, even while he was on Mount Sinai securing the holy tablets for their people. Not having Moses, even temporarily, meant for them no clear kinship with God, and so they had to have a viable substitute, akin to satisfying thirst and hunger. Such is the fragility of our Godly worship. It is our various religions and, yes, our many kinds of idols, which allow us to "see" God, this ever-invisible being "out there somewhere" for whom we (generally) have great affection. It is admittedly the strangest relationship possible, this human love for the invisible divine. Yet Moses was angry because his brethren could not forego having "someone to see" for even a little while. The Temple itself had become a kind of idol, yet ironically, idol worship largely abated during the Babylonian exile and the destruction of their first Temple, around 586 BCE. After the Maccabean revolt in the mid-2nd Century BCE, there evolved a fresh sense of the Jewish messiah (*Mashiach*), which conjured some sort of warrior-like figure who would free the Jews from the oppressive stench of the Romans. The Jews could finally have their lives back, if only their *Mashiach* would come. This conjuring of a Savior would replace both their use of idols and (I would say) the need for the Temple itself, since such a man would likely prove more valuable than a building, no matter that it once contained the Ark of the Covenant, which, for me at least, is still a sort of idol. It is this evolving desire for their *Mashiach* to finally arrive that, in terms of the time frame, is an important aspect of why Jesus came when He did. His people were hungry to be spared more years of Roman oppression, but, as we know, Jesus was not quite who they had in mind. As many others have said, Jesus wanted to expand His fellow

Jews' sense of God's holiness from merely a cherished building toward He who would embody such votive fervor Himself. Jesus' prediction that their second Temple would be destroyed within the next generation (forty years —in 70 CE) amplified His vision of how a life of service to others would prove to be more useful than mere animal sacrifices and compulsively obeying their many, many dietary and religious laws. Jesus thus told His fellow Jews that *there is more to our faith than everything you have known* for at least the past 1,200 years, and, in particular, *don't think I am your next idol.*

Most of us are familiar with at least the basic outlines of Jesus' ministry. He got baptized in the Jordan River by John the Baptist, began to preach and t each, and eventually, the healings and the miracles started to come. There were other teacher-preacher-healers at the time, but most of them have become only names in history books compared to Him. What about Jesus' miracles? All of them were important, both as events themselves as well as what they meant for His larger purpose, differing one to another. Many were singular but some affected thousands of people at a time. Some or many people came to see Jesus only to witness or even experience one of His miracles, and soon He too became familiar with this sentiment, and sometimes chastised them. Clearly, Jesus was no "living idol." For the first time in Judaism's long history, one of their own was not only receiving and obeying the Commandments (Moses), building a Temple (Solomon) or complaining about the Jews' chronic sinfulness and idolatry (virtually all of the Old Testament prophets). Jesus basically said *I am offering you something new, here and now, so what you do say?* It was His miracles that told His brethren that the hand of God was finally present, telling each other *What man alone can do such things?* These miracles were the beginning of both the popular confusion about Jesus as well as sowing the seeds of His eventual demise. Too soon, He became "not quite one of them," akin to a "spiritual stranger," which never really stopped.

*

Whether His disciples, the Pharisees or common people, no one was immune to Jesus' miracles. Every Jew shared a sense of what "God was like," according to generations of their faith. Jews have always quarreled about aspects of their religion, yet it was and is coherent and familiar to them. Jews have never had the denominational rancor of Christian Protestants, which I have come to find unnecessarily human vis-à-vis "what God is all about." While Jews accepted that miracles occurred and there was an after-life, these were not serious preoccupations for them, nor what they concerned themselves with or argued about. Only the Sadducees did not believe in resurrection, though this was not a real source of contention within the religious elite. Jews shared a common historical and religious system which, in practice, altered little for at least 1,200 years before Jesus, and neither did He wish to change it much, saying *"I have come to fulfill the Law."* Miracles, then as now, were not a subject of great religious discussion, and so when His miracles started coming, everyone's heads turned, the world suddenly changed, and God's divinity became plainer.

Although the Gospels describe Jesus' miracles coming somewhat regularly, we really don't know how often they occurred over perhaps the three years of His ministry. There were all the healing miracles, one feeding miracle and the resuscitation miracles. Each miracle provoked varying reactions amongst the common people, the disciples and the Pharisees. Each and every person could not avoid being profoundly affected by Jesus' miracles in the sense that "no reaction at all" was not possible, akin to being in a hurricane or tornado. Miracles are *spiritual weather*, they necessarily affect us, transcending any religion or understanding of how life works. Miracles are what spread Jesus' fame the quickest and the loudest, since "everyone's talking" about them. Miracles are not gossip, but they prove to be contagiously ripe like the juiciest gossip. So how did these various groups receive Jesus' miracles?

Common people, whether unfamiliar with Jesus or even those who had seen Him before, would have been utterly dumb-founded by His miracles. As we know, they sought Him out to be healed of all sorts of maladies, experiencing the eclipse of Judaic religion and entering the divine realm of God, to acutely sense the majesty of the universe. This is not my hyperbolic non-sense — this is what actually happens to people, since miracles affect us like nothing else. We know the crowds pressed upon Jesus to the point that sometimes he would have to escape them to rest for a while. He fleshed out what John the Baptist had been telling them beforehand, and now they knew that John had neither exaggerated or lied. Jesus was the true miracle worker, without question, that much they came to understand, and so they followed Him wherever He went. The Gospels state *"He healed all those who came to Him."* Jesus, though, wondered aloud *"will they stick with Me."*

The Pharisees were another matter. I sense that they struggled with Jesus' healing miracles (the man born blind, for example), but more so the raising of Lazarus (both: John's Gospel) in particular, because no dead person had ever been successfully resuscitated before — even on the fourth day after Lazarus had died. I think it was the raising of Lazarus that truly provoked the spiritual envy of the Pharisees, even beyond the crowds and Jesus' evolving fame. It was something quite inexplicable on any religious level, they could not consult the Torah for guidance, and there was no point arguing about whether His miracles were real or not: they were, and they knew it. Even more so than Jesus' over-turning the money-changers' tables a few days later at the Temple, the raising of Lazarus provoked an envious rage in the Pharisees that would permit only one "solution": to kill Him, because this was not only Judaism itself, this was truly God's work, which they clearly were not ready to receive, despite some 1,200 years of practice. There are no religious doctrines or customs when it comes to miracles. The world had utterly changed, and the Pharisees knew in a certain sense that they were no longer needed so much. Jesus now "owned" them, He had become what Freud called *ego alien* for them, and so, *He would have to die.*

Jesus' disciples were yet another matter altogether, and present us with the clearest situation psychologically regarding His miracles, given their constant proximity to His ministry. Conjure yourselves in the daily company of an unexpected miracle-worker over years of time. Each miracle and its situation was at least a little unique, even on the days when Jesus would heal people for hours until He grew too tired to continue. You as His disciples would undoubtedly talk amongst yourselves as to what might be going on. You would be regularly faced with God's obvious divinity, for which we are never truly prepared to witness. There would be no "reasonable" answers to your questions about how this was occurring, beyond platitudes about "God's Will." The miracles would always be freshly perplexing, as though you are being slapped in the face at any time by someone you could never see. It becomes more than slightly traumatic, in a good way, but there are never enough explanations, which leaves you confused and wondering *who is this God we have been searching for all these centuries, and what is He really like after all*? Remember, the miracles are always different, and never make complete sense, except that they are *necessary*. This goes on and on, day after month, which I think both excites and wears down the disciples over time, because the divine nature of Jesus' miracles never makes enough sense to mortal humans who, after all, were previously struggling to make a living and some sense of their Jewish lives under constant Roman oppression. The chasm between the earthly and the divine never really shrank for them, and Jesus was constantly "upping the ante," with new teachings to digest, and eventually the worst news: *He would die on the cross, largely at the hands of their fellow Jews.* So psychologically, I do not fault their chronic confusion or some of them sleeping in Gethsemane while Jesus prayed and asked God to relieved of His deathly burden. We would do no better. It was the miracles which drenched all those who came into contact with Jesus with the never-quite-edible phenomenon of *this is what God is all about*, and all religion became background.

In our own time, some of us ask God for (usually) healing miracles, and we are overjoyed when they (too rarely) happen. We have learned from Jesus' disciples not to be afraid of God anymore, since we better than they know "the end of His story." Better late than even later.

August 2021

WHAT ARE CHRISTIANS TO MAKE OF JUDAISM?

For several years, I have been interested in aspects of Judaism as they impact our Christian faith, since we will always be indebted to the Jews for not only the birth, life and resurrection of Jesus Christ, but also for gifting us their necessary monotheism to make His mission and purpose at all possible. Drawing upon two previous essays, I want to try to define the nature of Judaism for myself as a Christian who left the church eight years ago, working to clarify and thus deepen my faith journey since then. I have come to dislike the chronic chasm between Christians and Jews for the principal reason that this was not God's intention with bringing Jesus into our world, that Christians and Jews both chronically misunderstand each other, and, as someone else said, if there is going to be a Second Coming of Jesus, it will likely not happen until Jews also accept Him as their *Mashiach*, or Messiah. Could it really be true — after twenty centuries — that some or many Jews still do not know that Jesus, His disciples and their broader religious milieu were all Jewish? For their sakes, I hope not.

I want to present a brief history of Judaism as I (admittedly) barely understand it, certainly not at the level of its (overly) complex practices, nor its social culture, since I am obviously not Jewish. Out of this comes the old, thorny question of by whose motives and reasons Jesus was crucified as well as why Jews still do not accept Him as their *Mashiach*. There are limitations to Judaism as a religion, especially on a psychological level, which have greatly hindered such acceptance. There is also the reality that, while some Christians visit Israel (as I recently considered, but decided against pursuing) to better understand this Jewish background, many more Christians have really no working familiarity with Judaism beyond ubiquitous church-talk about "the ancient Israelites." It is frankly very easy for Christians to forget about Jews altogether. Growing up, I lived a half-mile from a synagogue for my entire childhood, yet it never came up in general conversation. The early Christian writer, Justin Martyr, among others, was ridiculing Jews as "superstitious" as early as the mid-2nd Century CE. After the Council of Nicaea in 325CE, Constantine separated Passover from Easter, saying Jews were "afflicted with blindness of soul" from their "enormous sin." An early Church father, John Chrysostom, discouraged Christians from attending synagogues and Jewish festivals. Various Catholic edicts forbade the use of Jewish materials in worship or to even eat with Jews. Three years before he died, Martin Luther wrote a vitriolic, anti-Jewish essay which was later used by Hitler to persecute Jews in Nazi Germany. I am not going to deal with the increate Jewish complaints against Christians regarding our recurring persecutions against them, since we are guilty as charged. This overly sour relationship between Christians and Jews is both mutual and deeply ingrained, representing the displacement of much acrimonious history onto each other from so long ago. It resembles a chronically distrustful divorced couple who must still raise their under-age children together. I will come around to their very current situation near the end, but first, a bit of Jewish history.

*

The origins of Judaism as described in the Torah are certainly at least partly historically accurate, and reflect a necessary spiritual story for the Jews to understand their singular beginnings as God's "chosen" monotheistic people. Judaism likely evolved over a lengthy period from Canaanite and other neighboring polytheistic religions, which already had both festivals and animal sacrifices. Both *Yahweh* and *Baal* (familiar names in the Old Testament) were Canaanite gods of weather and fertility which became central figures in the early Jewish evolution toward monotheism. As we know, there were originally twelve tribes of Jews, ten of which were lost due to domination by the Assyrians in 722 BCE. Complaints by many of the OT prophets (especially Jeremiah, who referred to his fellow Jews as "stupid children") centered on idol worship and sinfulness from these "other gods." Aron's creation of "the golden calf" while Moses was on Mount Sinai (for forty days) highlighted the Jewish emotional difficulty of retaining a purebred religion. Three annual festivals also evolved — Passover in the springtime, Sukkot (the feast of Tabernacles) celebrating the harvest in the autumn, and Hannukah late in the year, a remembrance of the Seleucid war in ca. 165 BCE. Messianic Jews, perhaps correctly, speculate that Jesus was born not in December, but at either Passover or Sukkot. The Jewish prohibition against eating pork may also have been derived from these other religions. While aspects of "the Jewish story" had been orally discussed for centuries, it was during the Babylonian exile (586-539 BCE), when many of the Jewish elite were taken out of the country, hence the fear of "losing their religion" became acutely worrisome, and what became the Old Testament (*Tanakh*) was written down in earnest. Idol worship eventually attenuated after this period, because the Jews now had something they could literally hold in their hands: a book about themselves which they had written. The Gospels would later be written against the backdrop of the destruction of the second Temple by the Romans in 70 CE to preserve oral stories about Jesus and the disciples as the Jews were banned in Jerusalem and scattered into the Diaspora. No one wants to be forgotten.

Thus came the merging of two "states of being" which would continue to define the Jews until our present time: multiple conquests by various invaders (including their Temple being twice destroyed), leading to their sense of not only being "set apart" by God, but a quite realistic persecution / slavery complex, this sentiment against their own Achilles' heel: a self-obsession with maintaining their religious integrity at all costs against any others, which would eventually bring about the Pharisees' conflicts with and the eventual death of Jesus Christ. Once the *Tanakh* was finalized, Judaism became a "book religion," and in the *Tanakh* we can more than glimpse the complexity of their religious practices in some detail, include the exacting mathematics for the construction of the Temple in 1 Kings 6:2-6 and 2 Chronicles 3:1-4. Later on would come the *Talmud* and *Mishnah* as written elaborations of the *Tanakh*, overseen by rabbis who "understood it all." Christianity simply has no equivalent to these books, as the hollower dogmas of the Catholic church are tame by comparison. The Jews had evolved a religious lifestyle that will never be duplicated, and it sinks them to too great a degree. What women have to do at Passover alone, in terms of cooking and cleaning, is wearying just to read. In Judaism, there are difficult-to-pronounce names for everything, and to remain "Torah-observant" is strenuous on one's time and temperament. It is certainly not for everyone — not even all Jews.

From this unfairly brief history, we can see that Judaism's pagan roots expose it to a certain problem: how much difference does it make to learn and yearly perform these ritual practices, to memorize so much Scripture and to cling so tightly to each other in an evolving modern world, where even "keeping Kosher" has significantly declined in our lifetime. How would Jews explain foregoing eating pork biologically, for example, as a source of protein, since they are not usually vegetarians? Animal sacrifices are pagan regardless of the religion, and so do not meaningfully further God's work. The 613 laws of Judaism became the skeletal cohesion of how to live God-centered lives, but, despite complaints to the contrary, obedience to such laws was and is a major Jewish preoccupation, while at least a few Jews will whisper that they long for a "personal relationship" with God enjoyed by (some) Christians. Paul's stress on the necessity of circumcision for the Jews did not explain its psychologically dubious value when dealing with our still-invisible God, then or now — it simply provides no real spiritual relief. While we can admire their devotion, what was and is gained merely by either animal sacrifices or obedience to the Law alone? How does any of this affect Jewish spirituality, and, if so, does this remain too much at the "idea level?" Judaism wobbles at the risk of being *mere religion*, however monotheistically so. It is clear that Jews themselves were looking for more during the period between the Seleucid War and the arrival of Jesus — whether a *Mashiach* or not — that obeyance to the Law was not enough under worsening Roman oppression, and so what would become of them? I will return to this after answering "the thorny question" mentioned earlier.

*

In a familiar story common to all four Gospels, we find Jesus intentionally damaging the money-changers' tables in the outer court of the Temple, the only place there where Gentiles were allowed to gather. In John's Gospel, this episode occurred during the first of three Passovers when He came up to Jerusalem, thus quite early in His ministry, rather than during Passion Week, as described in the Synoptics. John would have us see this as Jesus' introduction to the Jewish religious elite, likely evoking at least some animosity. Jesus famously replied that He could raise the Temple in three days if it was destroyed. This initiated an on-going dispute between Jesus and the Pharisees throughout much of this Gospel over His ministry, and whether He had real authority from God to pursue His mission. Also early on in this intra-Jewish discussion came Nicodemus, who, as a member of the Sanhedrin, wanted to better understand Jesus. Nicodemus' comrade in this pursuit was Joseph of Arimathea, who provided the tomb for Jesus' burial. Although John pejoratively called the Pharisees and Sadducees "the Jews," is there not some sincere curiosity about Jesus mixed in with their admittedly deceptive questions? At one point, they exasperatedly say "If this man were not from God, He could not do anything." (John 9:33). Others have pointed out the geographical contrast: the religious leaders were, of course, from Jerusalem, while Jesus and the disciples were from Galilee, which was famously ridiculed by Nathanael among others for being culturally backward. Jesus was always presenting Himself as a surprise to everyone, for better and worse, so what was it that truly rankled "the Jews" against Him over time, to the point of apparently wanting to kill Him?

Not being Catholic, with ecumenical popes who have wanted to appease the Jews for their role in Jesus' crucifixion, I do fault them for their participation in His death, even if God knew it was coming anyway. Do I fault all the Jewish people for all time — no, of course not. It was Caiaphas and some or most of the seventy members of the Sanhedrin who made their decision to press Pontius Pilate for Jesus' crucifixion, and who may have stirred up the crowd concerning Barrabas. They had a mutually beneficial relationship with the Roman government to maintain law and order in exchange for generally being left alone to practice their religion unperturbed. Jesus became a mystery to them, and the Sanhedrin were not — with two known members as exceptions — a spiritually curious bunch. In fairness, they did keep questioning Jesus to justify their eventual actions over perhaps as long as two years, and during that time, made no serious attempts to have Him arrested. The simplest reason for the religious elite's distaste for Jesus was that He did not appeal to their overly standardized version of Judaism, especially how it was being actualized in the Temple, a sentiment shared with the Essenes. Not the animal sacrifices or festivals, but rather the larger purpose of their religion had long been co-opted by human tendencies of power, rigidity and occasionally greed. *Judaism had already become stale*, but no one before Jesus knew what to do about it. The Pharisees and Sadducees felt pestered by Jesus (as Herod Antipas had by John the Baptist) for their moral shallowness and recurring spiritual hypocrisy, but even if they agreed with Him, they had no remedy in mind. People tend to get angry when they are criticized and even agree with the complaints, yet bristle when asked for any solutions. The learned religious elite, who prized their erudite opinions on Jewish matters, were, in essence, spiritually stumped, as they still are, as are most of the clergy in general. Whom else besides Jesus has God actually talked to since Moses? It would be easier for the Jewish elite to kill Jesus than be regularly reminded they had run out of gas as the spiritual mentors of their own people.

With this sentiment as an on-going irritant against Jesus, then came several situations as described in the Gospels which make His demise at the hands of the Jews more likely. While Pontius Pilate was certainly not an innocent party (he was removed from office in 36 CE for excessive cruelty to the populace), his knowledge of Jesus would likely have been peripheral at best. The religious leaders were getting ongoing reports about Jesus' mission when He was in Galilee and would be freshly apprised of Him during the festivals in Jerusalem. This mixture of curiosity and irritation about Jesus would simmer off and on over a lengthy period of time, with sudden bursts of seemingly divine qualities, either from Jesus' teachings or miracles. To use the old phrase, Jesus would "turn everyone's heads" with parables, lengthy discourses and, most keenly, miraculous healings. This being a "surprise to everyone," including His disciples, left everyone else confused and yet hopeful that God had finally sent them someone to raise their lives higher. Over and over, Jesus' work would press the limits of what His disciples, the Jewish populace and the religious elite could tolerate. Could Jesus actually be sent from God, as some sort of divine being? On and on this went for day after month for two or three years until the one episode occurred that transcended anything anyone had ever witnessed: the raising of Lazarus. If the chronology in John's Gospel is correct, Jesus' ministry was bracketed by the money-changers' tables near the beginning and the raising of Lazarus just before Passion Week. Jesus thus "provoked" His arrest by being a miraculous trouble-maker for the seeming benefit of a Jewish people who were being asked by Him to bend everything they knew into a new direction, all the while telling them the world may well end soon. It must have proven to be excitingly exhausting. In addition, since the Sadducees (who made up the majority of the Sanhedrin) did not believe in the resurrection of the dead, they would not have understood Jesus' statements about "raising the Temple in three days." The religious leaders' simmering emotionality came to a boil because yes, Jesus may have been more influential than they were, but, more importantly, they envied His miracles as the sign that God had brought Him forth into the world, which rendered them seemingly irrelevant — that was their fear. It was this envy of His miracles, with His power to raise the dead, that finally got Jesus killed. He simply wore them out, and this provoked "a circle of disbelief," including both Jesus' disciples as well as the Sanhedrin. They killed Jesus in the same way that His disciples fell asleep repeatedly in Gethsemane. There is something about witnessing miracles that sways us either toward a greater acceptance of a divine God or shuts down our belief in Him, perhaps altogether. Nearly everyone had had enough. Was Jesus surprised? Yes and no.

*

As we know, most of the original followers of Jesus were Jewish. This continued to be true through the rest of the 1st Century CE, though Gentiles became increasingly predominant as time went on. The main shift toward a largely Gentile-based Christianity accelerated during the 2nd Century CE onward, until rather few Jews remained involved. Both the static nature of Judaism as well the skepticism of the Sanhedrin about Jesus won out over a quasi-divine being whose life and mission were no longer cherished by those who had witnessed Him, since all of them had died. John the Evangelist was perhaps the last person claiming first-hand experience with Jesus, and, as someone else has said, how could His miracles truly be taught to those who could never witness Him. We all had to be there, and we still do — there was and is no substitute. That is why Christians wear crosses around our necks, it is as close as we will ever get to His crucifixion.

From the 2nd Century CE until the 1970s, there would be no significant influx of Jews becoming interested in Jesus as a religious figure, and certainly not as their *Mashiach*. There has always been a tiny cohort of "believers" in Israel and elsewhere, but such people were singularly independent in their Jewish faith and remained marginalized. I heard a YouTube testimonial by an Israeli recently who comes from a family of five generations of "believers" — quite unusual. The social psychology of Jews has always been to reduce Jesus to a "bad history lesson" who has no relevance to them, and that such "believers" are really Christians and not "true Jews." It is important to note that Jews have long been discouraged from reading the New Testament, and familial pressure to renounce Jesus was and is quite strong, including being disowned due to "conversion." When Jews start reading the Gospels, they often can not stop, and this usually forms the basis for their "conversion," some or many having been introduced to the NT by Christian friends or co-workers. Rabbis seem to be rarely consulted. If one member of a family "converts," others tend to follow. The greatest mystery about Christianity is how it survived at all, especially before Constantine's making it an official religion in the Roman Empire, largely due to his mother Helena's own conversion. Scholars have not quite explained this well enough, but its answer certainly has relevance for our own time.

Messianic Judaism began in the early 1970s in the United States as "Jews for Jesus," an organization still based in San Francisco. It is not clear to me how this began, but Messianic synagogues started cropping up perhaps 20-30 years ago around our country, and embody a typically

Jewish identity: they meet for *Shabbat* on Friday nights or Saturday mornings, their services employ music and dancing, with much praise of Israel. They do, of course, discuss Jesus and NT Scripture, and thus seek to blend the Old and New Testaments as the Biblical basis for their faith. The Eucharist or Communion is generally celebrated on a monthly basis, although they do not accept the Trinity. They do not celebrate Christmas, considering it to be a pagan rite outgrown from the ancient Roman festival of Saturnalia. Gentiles visit sometimes, and some actually convert. Thus they have rounded their Jewish identity with the revelation that Jesus Christ is the son of God, the Anointed One, *for them*. In a sense, this Messianic Judaism has come out of nowhere, yet it takes them back to 1st Century Israel, the disciples and the earliest churches. There are also Internet sites in Israel devoted to bridging the chasm between the Jews and *Yeshua* (Jesus). After all this time, these "believers" have leaped over so much acrimonious history to "do a new thing," and it is truly a blessing for all of us. While still unpopular among Jews generally, they have finally discovered the real purpose of their religion: to be the spiritual midwife of our beloved *Mashiach*.

In December 2015, a group of Orthodox rabbis issued a *Statement on Christianity*, offering to work together with Christians after recognizing our value in "seeking to do the Will of our Father in Heaven," appreciating the hand extended by the Catholic church through Vatican II in the 1960s. They also alluded to "the unique relationship between Christians and Jews," having "experienced sincere love and respect from many Christians." Christianity "is neither an accident nor error, but the willed divine outcome and gift to the nations." Jesus, it goes on, ended idol worship, and Christians have read and studied the *Tanakh* for divine revelation. And then: "neither of us can achieve God's mission in this world alone." If this is not Jewish forgiveness for all the mistreatment suffered at the hands of Christians over the centuries, it is certainly generous. Not surprisingly, they do not wish to receive our proselytizing, but some Jews have already willingly done so, as described above.

Could there be a church / synagogue service involving Protestants, Catholics and Messianic Jews, led by clergy and which combine elements of all three groups, as an experiment in inter-faith amity? It is long past time to allow Jesus Christ to be the magnetic core for both Christians and Jews, since that is what God intended to happen on Luke's wondrous night in Bethlehem, so long and longer ago.

November 2021

A SORT OF SCRIPTURAL DIAMOND
(The Gospel of John)

Despite being raised as a Presbyterian, attending Sunday School both as a child and adult, and being regularly involved for many years in the church, until the past few years, I had only rarely read the Bible. I had quickly read through the entire Bible more than 30 years ago, but did not study what I had read to any real degree. Many church-goers would call me Biblically illiterate, and thus barely a Christian at all. During earlier years I have since been uninvolved in church, pursuing Scripture did not interest me enough to take the time to read or study it seriously. I think this is true for too many people, perhaps even the majority of Christians. Church attendance is too often deemed to be enough: an hour or two on (some) Sundays, then the rest of week must be lived otherwise. There is too little time, it seems, for reading our beloved Bible.

Several years ago, I bought a newly translated version of the New Testament by an American scholar, wound up reading it entirely, and then did so (again) with the Old Testament (what Jews call the *Tanakh*. More recently, I re-read the OT prophets to see if I had missed anything important. So, I read the entire Bible within a figurative blink of an eye, considering how old I am. That I only feel a little embarrassed in saying this reflects a commonplace fact: too many Christians do not have more than a cursory understanding of the Bible, and too many of us are fine with this. While the Bible is well-known and well-sold, it is not necessarily many peoples' favorite book. I have probably read the OT at length as much as I care to, since, for me, it primarily belongs to the Jews, and the rest of us borrow it mostly for its relevance to Jesus. While the OT prophecies about Jesus are interesting, they pale in comparison to what we learn about Him in the Gospels. Aspects of Isaiah and Jeremiah in particular do seriously interest me. I find the Book of Revelation to be overly hyperbolic, and frankly not useful. Paul's work is of greater interest, though he labors over some points too much. The Gospels of Matthew and Luke are too derivative (I really mean *plagiaristic*) of Mark's Gospel to be truly anymore helpful, aside from the Sermon on the Mount, the Beatitudes and Luke's birth narrative of Jesus, if it is indeed historically true. Which primarily leaves me with Mark's and John's Gospels, the Book of Acts and, secondarily, Paul. So, even after reading the whole Bible, I have become (too) picky about what inspires and keeps me curious.

My evolving fondness for John's Gospel began rather accidently. I got an email from a Baptist seminary offering a free on-line course on this Gospel, so I listened to it, but found it lacking much substance, despite being taught by the president of the seminary. This soon led me to read books by several authors, including a two-volume scholar's commentary which covered the entire Gospel, line by line, with much background material provided on its 1st Century Jewish context. I realized that I had to re-read Mark's Gospel, because its simpler nature, akin to journalistic "reportage" of Jesus' life and mission, serves as a clearer introduction to John's more spiritual language. I have come to see Mark's and John's Gospels as a "curious pair," and indeed, some Biblical scholars are persuaded that John had at least a working familiarity with Mark's Gospel, and perhaps all three Synoptics. John's material is about 85% distinct from the Synoptics, as though he wished to provide "the rest of the story" about Jesus. I have personally concluded that John's Gospel is the most important book in the Bible, but, without Mark's Gospel, it does not make enough sense. John's has been called "the spiritual Gospel," but it is not that simple. In the past 50 or so years, scholars have re-examined this Gospel to better appreciate its unique qualities in telling the story of Jesus. So, quite accidentally, it has become my favorite, and I have now read it several times. It is a Biblical, spiritual diamond of sorts, which I will explain.

*

Of all the Gospels, John's is probably the most controversial and the least well-understood. Biblical scholars often disagree about many of its aspects: even, after all these centuries, who wrote it and when. Possible authors include: (most commonly) John the Apostle, son of Zebedee, often considered to be "the Beloved Disciple" in this Gospel;

a shadowy figure named John the Elder, based in Jerusalem, who was a follower of Jesus; the disciple Thomas, or even Lazarus. Few other candidates are taken seriously. Dating the Gospel to ca. 90-95 CE is a general scholarly consensus, placing it later than any of the Synoptics. One problem with such a late date is that either the Apostle John and/or the Beloved Disciple (whether one or two different people) would have been quite old by that time, particularly in antiquity. Theories of one, two or three editions of the Gospel have been proposed. There is a vague reference to the death of the Beloved Disciple quite late in the Gospel, such that a secondary author or "redactor" might have finished it as a sort of ancient ghost writer. One point that everyone agrees on is the clear sense that this Gospel is based on someone's eyewitness testimony, certainly more so than in the Synoptics. While Peter was consulted in writing Mark's Gospel, he did no writing of his own, and Jon Mark was free to recollect Peter's stories about Jesus as he wished. In John's Gospel, Jesus speaks at greater length more regularly, to the degree that it is likely someone is writing His words down, much like a modern-day stenographer. The level of His abstract reasoning in the "Farewell Discourses" (chapters 14-16) becomes too complex to be simply remembered, however accurately. For the first time in the Gospels, we have a clearer sense of how Jesus sounds, less edited yet still elusive. Scholars generally divide this Gospel into "The Book of Signs" (chapters 1-12) and "The Book of Glory" (chapters 13-21) to highlight both the practical and spiritual aspects of Jesus' ministry.

In contrast to the year-long time frame of Jesus' ministry in the Synoptics, in John's Gospel Jesus attends three Passovers (*Pesach*) as well as (perhaps) Pentecost (*Shavuot*), the autumnal Feast of the Tabernacles (*Sukkot*) and *Hanukkah* (the Feast of Dedication) one time each. Hence, His mission lasts some two to three years. The sense of chronology is less clear, and Jesus travels back and forth from Galilee to Jerusalem as well as venturing into Samaria, where He is surprisingly well-received. The Samaritans had long-held grievances against their fellow Jews in Judea, due to their belief that their own Temple on Mount Gerizim was the "real" Temple location deserving of worship, so the two groups of Jews did not fraternize. We briefly hear from other disciples about who Jesus might be, and how could Nazareth produce a prophet of His apparent magnitude. Chapters are quite varied, with little obvious continuity between them until Passion Week. We hear Nicodemus' perplexity over being "born again." There are many singular vignettes that make for interesting reading. In contrast to the hurried pace of Mark's Gospel, with its murky ending regarding Jesus' resurrection, John's pace is slower as our picture of Jesus steadily evolves. There are no parables, there is no "official" Last Supper and no angst in Gethsemane, though there are miracles ("signs"), such as the raising of Lazarus, and there is, above all, the Beloved Disciple's finding what we now call the Shroud of Turin and the Sudarium of Oviedo in Jesus' tomb. We also get a better sense of the local topography and of Jewish culture. It has become my delight to read and re-read, as it is where Jesus more readily comes alive.

*

I will provide a general overview of John's Gospel, with some personal commentary. Bear in mind, as with the rest of the Bible, it is a mixture of historical facts, embellishments of such facts and some possible outright fabrication. As many others have mentioned, the Bible is not a history textbook, as the ancients did not so easily distinguish between fact and fiction. The mythological stories of Adam and Eve in the Garden of Eden, the Exodus and Noah's flood are indeed useful as an explanatory means of understanding how the world worked to them. I otherwise in no way accept the inerrancy of the Bible — it was written by men inspired by God, but not God Himself, as He did not have to write, having created the universe. I will take up John's Prologue near the end of the discussion, and so begin with Jesus' well-known culinary triumph: turning water into wine.

What is important about the wedding at Cana is that Mary makes a sort of motherly demand of Jesus that He is not ready to fulfill, as His ministry has at most barely begun, yet He appeases her out of sense of a son's duty. This revelation has no relevance to the sort of healing miracles which come later, yet the episode, in John's words, "made His glory manifest" (2:11). John places Jesus' destruction of the money-changers' tables quite early in his Gospel, which could explain why "the Jews" (who represent the religious elite, and not the general Jewish populace) are already incensed and want to kill Him. Scholars have questioned how big a stir this incident would have caused within the huge courtyards of the Temple, though the episode must have aroused more than a little consternation. During this first of three Passovers, Jesus begins to draw crowds and develop a following. John's theme of light and darkness (also a motif for the Essenes) is discussed with Nicodemus, and that "God's ire" will rest upon those who reject Jesus as God's Son. While the woman at the well in Samaria does accept Jesus, He reminds her that "salvation is from the Judeans" (4:22) as she and her own people await the coming of their *Mashiach*, so Jesus stays with them for two days. Rejected by His own people in Nazareth, Jesus becomes based across Galilee, often in Capernaum and sometimes in Cana, while continuing to visit Jerusalem for the annual festivals. John correctly describes the pool at Bethesda, with its five porticos (as confirmed archaeologically), where Jesus heals a man lame man on the Sabbath, which riles up the Pharisees for equating Himself with God. While there is the sense that Jesus is indeed seeing Himself in God's fold as (at least) His Son, He repeatedly says that He is subservient to God, hence I see this as no endorsement on His part of a Trinitarian posture. There are differing versions of "the Son can do nothing from Himself, except what He sees the Father doing" (5:19) sprinkled throughout this Gospel, and most clearly: "Of Myself, I can do nothing. If I testify concerning myself, my testimony is not true" (5:31). Rather, Jesus equates Himself more directly with Moses, "in whom you had hoped" (5:45). Jesus' preferred name for Himself will come soon enough.

As His healings become better-known, Jesus feeds the 5,000 and walks upon the water to impress His frightened disciples that He is indeed a divinely-transfused being. He tells the crowds about "having descended from Heaven to do the will of the One having sent Me" (6:38), and proposes that He is the new manna from Heaven for their eternal life. An early allusion to what we call the Eucharist is made, but proves confusing, even unbearable to His disciples and others. Jesus refers to

Himself as "*the Son of Man*," echoing the term from the Book of Daniel about a mysterious figure who comes to pronounce "the End of Days." Jesus attends *Sukkot* amidst hostility from the Pharisees, and we must remember that John's Gospel was written during a period when the Johannine community was also drawing the wrath of more traditional Jews, who wound up expelling them from the synagogues. Thus, John's use of "the Jews" is quite personal — Jews against Jews concerning whether their *Mashiach* had already come or not. Despite His statements and actions, Jesus continues to gain followers in Jerusalem, while others remain skeptical. Some scholars have noted the cultural divide between Jerusalem and Galilee, and it is true that Nazareth had no synagogue during Jesus' time, with at most several hundred inhabitants. The Pharisees demand that "a prophet is not raised up out of the Galilee" (7:52). The story of the woman caught in adultery is straight-forward, with Jesus drawing in the sand with His finger as He ponders what to do about her. He soon drops the bomb that will provoke much Pharisaic wrath: "I tell you, before Abraham came to be, I AM" (8:58), leaving them frothing to stone Jesus then and there.

Next, a chapter-long story about Jesus healing a beggar blind from birth at the pool of Siloam, who is interrogated by the Pharisees, they wondering whether he is malingering, yet genuinely ask "How can a sinful man (Jesus, who again heals on the Sabbath) perform such signs?" (9:16). The beggar's parents are also questioned, but answer the Pharisees hesitantly, fearful they could be expelled from their synagogue. Under such questioning, the beggar asks the Pharisees "Do you wish to become His disciples?" ((9;27), to which they respond "We do not know where this man comes from" (9:29), summarizing their ongoing dilemma with Jesus until He is crucified. They do relent by saying "If this man were not from God, He could not do anything." (9:33). The beggar is then expelled from the synagogue by the insulted Pharisees, and Jesus later helps him to understand about His being *the Son of Man*. Spiritual wisdom sprouts from an unlikely source.

A second lengthy story concerns the familiar raising of Lazarus, Jesus' good friend, in Bethany, on His way to Jerusalem for what will become Passion Week. He purposely waits two extra days before arriving there to show Lazarus' sisters, Martha and Mary, that He is still capable of raising Lazarus after he has died, accompanied by His half-believing but curious disciples. Through Martha's faith that Jesus is indeed their long-sought *Mashiach*, Lazarus is raised on the fourth day, one day later than the usual Jewish burial customs are performed. This story foretells much about what will come later when Jesus is arrested, particularly Pontius Pilate's confusion over what to do about Him. More than anything else that happens, it is likely this episode that seals Jesus' fate, due to the ongoing Pharisaic wrath and fear of Roman intervention against them, now coupled with their worsening envy over Jesus' miracle-making.

Before the third *Pesach*, the Jewish religious leaders, admittedly envious of Jesus, now consider killing Lazarus after his being raised, as Jesus continues to gain the favor of other Jews who see

Him as "someone special." There is Palm Sunday, with Jesus riding on the donkey as foretold in Zechariah 9:9, as the Pharisees mutter: "The world has gone after Him." (12:19). Others continue to remain skeptical of Jesus, however, as He begins to allude to His ministry soon coming to a close. Knowing Judas Iscariot will soon betray Him, Jesus washes the disciples' feet to provide to them an example of servitude before predicting that all of them will soon betray Him. He tells them that where He is going, they can not follow Him, but promises "not to leave you orphans." (14:18). He will send to them "the Advocate," the Holy Spirit, who will "teach you everything," and not to be afraid. It is the beginning of the end, and, of course, the disciples are troubled. Philip asks to be shown God, but Jesus denies him, as was Moses denied, and a sense of foreboding ensues.

Four chapters can be summarized as what scholars have called *discourses*: Jesus speaking at greater length to His disciples about both what is to come as well as how they are to continue on without Him. These discourses are virtually never read or discussed in church, which is unfortunate, because they give us the clearest sense of how Jesus sees Himself and His ministry. John's use of what poets call "circular language" in his Prologue probably comes from these discourses, perhaps hearing this directly from Jesus in loving kinship with His disciples, to whom He is providing a kind of substantial "spiritual pep talk" for their work after He is gone. This is where the description of Jesus as "the good shepherd" comes from, which adorns the names of so many Protestant churches, calling Himself "the sheep's gate" (10:7). His followers ("sheep") will not follow "hirelings" (the Jewish religious elite), but only the shepherd who also has "sheep which are not from this fold" (the Gentiles), and so "there will come to be one flock, one shepherd" (10:16). His death and resurrection are again highlighted before being encircled by "the Judeans," asking Jesus "For how long are you going to keep a grip on our souls?" (10:24). Jesus replies that they "are not from among My sheep," (10:26), to which "the Judeans" again threaten to stone Him because "You are a man making yourself out to be God" (10:33). Jesus replies that He is indeed the Son of God. The "farewell discourses" consist entirely of Jesus telling the disciples about His relationship with God, telling them to keep the Commandments, and that the world "hates" Him, God and them. They will eventually be expelled from the synagogues, but that He must "go away" in order for "the Advocate" to come upon them. The disciples are understandably confused and "anguished," as Jesus will die and be resurrected "in a little while," while He tells them "I have conquered the cosmos" (16:33). At length, Jesus describes the singular purpose of His and their mission: to truly bring God into an oppressive and distrusting world. These "speeches" are given in place of the Last Supper as described in the Synoptics, using His holy words instead of sacramental bread and wine. It is not an "either/or" but "both" words and nourishment that Jesus provides as His encouraging them for the long journey ahead, too soon without Him. As I said earlier, I think someone is writing all of this down, because it is too memorable.

We then come to the arrest, trial and crucifixion of Jesus, and John's Gospel shares much in common with the Synoptics in this account, although some details are different. Peter cuts off Caiaphas' slave's ear when Jesus is arrested, and the Beloved Disciple is allowed to meet with Caiaphas, while Peter famously denies knowing Jesus three times.

It is nearly dawn when Jesus encounters Pilate, who finds "absolutely no case against Him" (18:38). While there is no historical confirmation of Pilate's authority to release a prisoner during *Pesach*, this appears in all four Gospels — but why would he want to release Barabbas, perhaps a zealot? After Jesus is flogged, Pilate still wants to release Him, but "the Judeans'" demand for Him to be crucified, telling Pilate "If you release this man, you are not a friend of Caesar" (19:12). Jesus then carries His own cross (no Simon of Cyrene) to Golgotha, where His mother, Mary, the Beloved Disciple and two other Marys (Mary' sister and Magdalene) watch Him get hammered to the cross. Jesus drinks hyssop to relieve His pain, but once dead, His legs are not broken, as is the typical Roman action during crucifixion. Joseph of Arimathea has Jesus placed in a new tomb, wrapped in linen cloths, which we now know were quite expensive.

Some 36 hours later, Mary Magdalene finds Jesus in an adjacent garden after Peter and the Beloved Disciple see the linen clothes in the empty tomb. Thus, He reveals Himself first to a weeping woman, who is disbelieved when she tells the disciples she has found their Master. Jesus later comes through the walls of the Upper Room, and Thomas proclaims his allegiance to Jesus as God's divine Son. In the last chapter, we find Jesus on the beach grilling fish, then revealing Himself to seven of His disciples, who have been fishing unsuccessfully, so He "helps them out" with a bursting catch of (exactly) 153 fish. In a scene I have never even heard mentioned in church but displays (for me) a sarcastic Jesus, He asks Peter three times: "Do you love Me?" and tells them that the Beloved Disciple "will not die," which is, of course, not true, though John lived to be quite old. Peter's own later crucifixion is also foretold. We are told "there are many other things that Jesus also did" (21:25), which only makes us curious, and there the story ends.

*

Why do I call John's Gospel "a sort of Scriptural diamond?" As can be seen, nearly each chapter presents new material, which ranges from specific episodes about individuals being healed to debates between Jesus and the Pharisees, and a large-scale feeding of thousands of people. The variety of material, combined with its intensely spiritual presentation, renders this Fourth Gospel as our primary lens through which to view Jesus as an increasingly divine man-god blessed by His holy Father with both a miraculous healing touch as well as wisdom beyond what we mere mortals can either conceive of or often fathom. It is diamond-like in its many-faceted portraits of Jesus doing the work of His ministry in various locales and with a variety of fellow Jews to provide evidence that indeed their *Mashiach* has finally come, He knowing that He will not be well-received and thus will ultimately die for His cause. Each chapter is its own story, and can be either read alone or in conjunction with others to sample the range of what is offered, akin to eating pieces of differently-flavored cakes in a dessert buffet. John's Gospel must come out of a personal experience of witnessing Jesus up close and then pondering this for perhaps decades, in the meantime learning sufficient Greek to be able to write it all down. It is the distilled wisdom of an older man who knows how fortunate he was to be allowed to walk with Jesus long enough to change his own life. It took me several readings of this Gospel before I could really appreciate its special qualities of both the ordinary and the divine, its crystalline wisdom and its singular surprise near the end.

That surprise? John 20:1-9 tells how the Beloved Disciple and Peter run to find the linen shrouds in the empty tomb. As I mentioned earlier, these are the Shroud of Turin and the Sudarium of Oviedo, which, through ongoing scientific analysis, are linked together by the same blood stain patterns and so belong to the same man. The Beloved Disciple "saw and believed" that Jesus was the *Mashiach* based on finding these cloths, despite the Shroud's faint appearance without the benefit of our magnification and photography. It is clear to him that Jesus' image has been imprinted on the cloth, and that God has done so. He thus literally holds divinity in his own hands, which could not be denied. It is this personally-held sentiment that forms the basis for John's famous Prologue, which is read in church every Christmas. John uses Jesus' own circular language from the Farewell Discourses to articulate a quasi-poetic summary of both his time with Jesus and the divine revelation startling him at the tomb. Even if Jesus is ultimately rejected by many of the Jews, God makes sure that His disciples do not do so. Thus, God's own greeting card.

I met a young man years ago who told me that he was an atheist. I asked if he was familiar with the Shroud, and he nodded affirmatively. When I asked what he thought of it, he admitted "I don't know about that," implying it could be genuine. It *is* genuine. Only in John's Gospel does Jesus so readily prove Himself to be who He says He is, and so the disciples respond: *"Now we know that You know all things. By this we have faith that You came forth from God." (*16:30*).*

January 2022

JUDAISM ECLIPSING UNTO JESUS CHRIST

Working from several of my previous essays, I want to try to encourage Judaism's practitioners to move beyond the static nature of their religion to embrace our rather obvious shared Messiah or *Mashiach*, Jesus Christ. From its beginnings, Christians have remained puzzled, resentful and, unfortunately, sometimes assaultive toward Jews for not "making the connection," but it was and is not so simple for them, who have been indoctrinated from the origins of Judaism to reject anyone who does not meet the requirements as outlined in their faith for such a divine presence. Thus, Judaism has stagnated over nearly 2,000 years, despite the *Mishnah* and T*almud*, which barely consider Jesus (*Yeshua*) at all, combined with the nay-saying about Him by Maimonides, their well-respected 12th Century rabbi. As I have mentioned before, too-few Jews have even read the New Testament, despite its being available (Jerome's Vulgate Bible, in Latin) since the 4th Century. Aside from my earlier brief review of the history of Judaism, I want to examine both its social psychology as well as what has to occur within this realm for the acceptance of Jesus to be better received, since it is not mere religion that holds them back. Having looked at Messianic Judaism as a recent development in this vein, I am concerned that this "sect" will not grow fast enough over time to persuade a sufficient number of Jews to accept Jesus, so that they will remain a spiritually languishing people perpetually searching for the true purpose of their particular faith. In other words, I almost feel sorry for them for whom they are missing. While Jeremiah called his brethren "*stupid children*" (4:22) for their tendency to engage in idol worship, this "stupidity" runs deeper than mere name-calling will fix. As Freud often said, we must deal with Jews' *resistance* to even look beyond what they know, which has become mere religion for its own sake. There was and is too strong a pagan tendency in Judaism, which gets in the way of seeking a Messiah more seriously. If Christians are grafted to the Jews' olive tree, can Jews eventually become grafted onto our *Mashiach*, seemingly before the end of time? It is true that many Christians simply do not know what to do with Jews, despite God's intent for us all to "swim in His river." Christian pilgrims visit Israel every year, to the extent that Jerusalem depends on tourist revenue, though such money "has not talked enough." American evangelicals might mutter "Can't they be saved," to which I answer, *still not yet*. Underneath Christian indifference to Jews can easily found the question: "What will it take?"

Every religion tries to deal with this same overarching central "problem": what to do about God's increate invisibility, as we all know that we will likely never see Him, even in Heaven. His famous white light, which ushers us toward His divine majesty in a realm beyond the simpler ease of our many speculative theologies and comparatively comical creeds and rituals, may be as close as we ever get from this side of the too-rarely bridgeable chasm between the human and the divine. Judaism, like any other religion, was developed by human beings, with our unmatched potential to guess at least half-wrongly about what God is like and how He might deal with us. Jews do know they were singularly chosen by God because He saw in them a surprising capacity to become monotheistically devoted to Him out of a cultural panoply of polytheistic gods, most of whom were notoriously fickle and hard to please for the simplest of things. God's covenant with Abraham and Moses, as described in the *Tanakh*, is a sometimes heroic story suggesting that they indeed were capable of remaining faithful to an unseen and untouchable being, despite their waywardness and corruption. For me, that is the greatest enduring strength of Judaism: that God did and does brand them as His chosen people for the purpose of that certain day granting them the brash favor of a humanly-lived *Mashiach* as His representative among us, and that He will not abandon them despite their many centuries of "stiff-necked" rebellion, idol worship and nearly incorrigible ability to misunderstand Him, having been gifted the only man-god ever born: Jesus Christ.

*

First, a bit different version of the history of Judaism than I described in a previous essay. The Jewish customs and rituals which I will examine shortly were developed over a long span of time to coax forth their single-minded spiritual posture of devotion unto God with the intent of trying to pull Him inside them to improve their moral lives, which Freud called *introjection*. This occurs when a person(s) or idea(s) are internalized to such a refined degree that our behavior readily reflects such influence(s). Culture itself is readily introjected to form social psychology, which, in Judaism, has generally taken the form of *us versus them*. Jews believe that God belongs to them, and the rest of us "borrow" Him for our own paler usage, because they are His chosen people. Most of us are rudimentarily familiar with basic Jewish rituals and practices: the Tabernacle in the desert and the later two Temples, animal sacrifices, dietary laws restricting what can be eaten, encouragement to almost obsessively (re-)read the *Tanakh*, and their three major annual festivals: Passover (*Pesach*), Pentecost (*Shavuot*) and the Feast of Tabernacles (*Sukkot)*. All of this forms a "spiritual bubble" in which Jews live to devote themselves to God through practicing their faith in this manner, and such, for too many Jews, this is enough. If they were asked about something like "the white light of Heaven," they would perhaps know of it, but it does not figure into their way-of-being. Judaism is a self-referential, even solipsistic system of beliefs and practices which remains stubbornly insular and so nearly indestructible. It preserves itself through a time-honored tradition, which only rarely gets challenged or disturbed, as when Jesus bristled at its limitations and was later harshly disparaged for doing so. The Temple served as a sort of religious clearing-house for all things Jewish, with its pilgrimages, baths for ritual purity and gold-plated milieu. The first Temple was built by Solomon in the 10th Century BCE, the second after the end of the Babylonian Exile in the 6th Century BCE. No attempt has been made to reconstruct a third Temple since it was destroyed by the Romans in 70 CE, and later I will answer why. Note that the *Mishnah* and *Talmud*, as detailed descriptions of the Jewish way of life, can not be taken from them. Judaism, after the Temples were destroyed, became a "book religion," with all the rigidities and disdain this implies.

Second, what these rituals and practices in Judaism mean from an outsider's perspective, and how they continue to hold the Jews back from God. Jeremiah and other Old Testament prophets lamented and shamed their brethren over indulging in idol worship, even while Moses spent forty days on Mount Sinai receiving the Ten Commandments from God. In fairness, they had been wandering in the desert for a long time, and could not have known what he was bringing them from the mountaintop. As I have discussed Jewish idol worship before, I will only say here that this was a necessary stepping-stone on their journey toward a working monotheism, which took centuries to be released into practice, since n*o one sees God*. It is hard to maintain religious devotion on a daily or yearly basis without some tangible reward, so I do not fault them so much for their entrenched idol worship. The cute little statues, such as for *Baal*, do look a bit silly, though. The Temple itself became a sort of stone-and-gold idol where certain things predictably happened which illustrated what Judaism thought God was doing in their favor. In the Temple's Holy of Holies, its innermost sanctuary, was the Ark of the Covenant, made from acacia wood and plated in gold. Only the high priest saw the Ark once a year, hence, when it was lost or destroyed after the second Temple was ruined in 586 BCE, the Jewish populace had never seen it, yet God "lived there." The Ark was a beautifully-crafted idol which had previously been carried into battle and was deemed to have special powers, and yet, when it was gone, God had not abandoned the Jewish people. Their dietary laws serve the function of pantheistic infusion of at least religion into inanimate foods to suggest that what we do or don't eat positively or adversely affects our spirituality, rather than merely sustains us biologically. When I eat pork or lobster, then not only have I sinned, but I also risk being cursed by God for blatantly disobeying Jewish Law for my own pleasure. This reminds us of Catholic transubstantiation during the Eucharist in Mass, when bread and wine supposedly become the literal body and blood of Jesus, although He never intended such a concretized interpretation to His disciples before being crucified. Circumcision, a covenant practice in Judaism, provides no real spiritual blessings for millions of male Christians. When I said earlier that Judaism can be overly pagan, this is what I mean. God is neither food or idols, He is not creeds or the Law, as He is the Creator of the universe. Let us always know the difference.

Third, there is psychological identity: one of the most important, steadfast qualities of our human functioning. Identity is both personal and familial as well as social and national. It cohesively binds us to our loved ones, our neighbors and countrymen, our sports teams, our politics and our religion (especially atheism, the most parasitic religion). Whether religious or not, Jews are an ethnic group with a shared cultural history dating back at least 3,500 years, along with familial, social and religious customs within a smaller geographical region. There are some 16-18 million Jews in our world of over eight billion people, and most of them live either in Israel or the United States. The history of their being persecuted by various groups is well-known, most egregiously by Christians, in terms of the sheer number of Jewish lives lost. Their hyper-sensitivity to insult and potential threats is also well-known, and, while understandable, cuts both ways. It is both protective of Jewish history and culture, but tends too often to be intolerant of new ideas out of their fear of again being subjugated by "foreigners," especially Gentiles. Traditional Jews attack their Messianic brethren in Israel for the nauseating proposition that Jesus is indeed their shared *Mashiach*, and have taken legal action to try to prevent the Messianic message from being heard there. How do we know that the Pharisees wanted to kill Jesus as described in the Gospels? Because traditional Jews today coerce their own ethnic brethren not to break ranks with them, as families in Israel disown their grown children for becoming believers in Jesus Christ. It is again the anguished cry of "Blasphemy!" My problem as a Gentile outsider with all of this is that it has little to do with God, as He cares about our religious preferences only so much — that we believe in Him, and do His work in this world. The thorny history of Jewish persecution can not be used as a perpetual excuse to avoid considering the obvious: that Jesus is the son of God. Judaism has, for 2,000 years, really travelled nowhere in any significant direction. It has wandered in circles for well longer than for forty years in the desert, and so strangely, Jesus has watched His fellow Jews do this wandering while He stands just out of sight, vexing and sighing, *every day*. Any Second Coming awaits their devoted participation with Him — not just studying the *Tanakh*, engaging in religious practices or assuring continued orthodoxy. Jews have always belonged to Him since the days of miracles in Galilee and Jerusalem, and when Mary Magdalene found Him alive outside the tomb. It is God whom they must seek, and not merely themselves.

*

If not the ancient Temples or the Ark of the Covenant, if not the dietary laws or animal sacrifices, the annual festivals or other rituals of Jewish life, then what of Judaism is left that maintains a real covenant with God? The answer lies in the difference between *what* and *whom*, between what can be eaten or read against who could be witnessed as surely more divine than any of the rest of us. It is the difference between a baby's pacifier and their mother, between an object and a person: that is the answer to this languishing Jewish dilemma as to the real purpose of their religion. Jews are very proficient at maintaining a religion, but any sense of the divine realm was and is only rarely considered, which is true of most religions. Christianity itself has also struggled with this, but at least we have a diviner figure upon whom to spiritually gaze. Catholicism borrowed Judaism's love of endless arguing about dogmas and heresies, which to a great degree, tainted its usefulness after the Council of Nicaea in the early 4th Century. Constantine thought God and Jesus could be decided upon by a group of several hundred clergymen, and so the matter would finally be settled after two hundred years of bickering amongst theologians. He was wrong, since it was and is never settled well enough for our collective liking. Messianic Judaism is now a heresy in Israel, though it probably will not be banished like so many dismissed Christian sects. So what would it take for more if not most Jews in Israel and America to accept Jesus as their *Mashiach?*

What verses *whom*. Religion verses spirituality, which sounds a bit strange, since doesn't religion lead to spirituality? Not necessarily. In American polling on religion, the current slogan tends to be "I'm spiritual, but not religious." I take this to mean such people have given up on church, but still believe in God, which, if true, would include me. Remember I mentioned the Freudian concept of therapeutic resistance, which is what it sounds like: an entrenched defensiveness about the patient's personal situation and why they might fear changing. We are all resistant about things in one way or another. I am not especially keen to learn how to use a smart phone, for example. I don't think we start with lending Scripture to people who are hesitant or resistant to hearing about Jesus. I myself don't like evangelicals spouting "Bible stuff" to me when I pass by them in public, as it is annoyingly presumptuous. We start with the resistible question: "What do you know about Jesus?" and then listen for how negative their reaction(s) are. The initial goal would be for traditional Jews to eventually say "I don't know much about Him," which, curiously, would be the best answer, because "I don't know" can become "I am surprised that He is not only whom I had heard about," implying animosity. The issue of *what* verses *whom* is broached as can traditional Jews not exactly set aside their bias against Jesus (no, certainly not initially), but can they even entertain any discussion at all that is not dismissively punitive? The social psychology of Judaism tends to be to dismiss what falls outside common knowledge and practice, and some aspects of cult psychology are present. Telling such Jews to go home and read the Gospels would likely be asking too much, too soon. They will say He does not matter — so what would matter to them?

We could ask them "What is the purpose of Judaism for God?" They would recite the *Shema*, reflecting the historic Jewish covenant with

God from Mount Sinai, into which we slip a slight complication: "Jesus is God's human reflection of the Shema's covenant, He is part of the oneness of God for the Jews." They would vigorously shake their heads, to which we answer "Did not Jesus perform miracles, and how would He do so without authority from God." The wonderful line from John 9:32, out of the mouths of the Pharisees, then gets quoted: "*If this man were not from God, He could not do anything.*" We have to nudge them toward the outskirts of Judaism to say "What you have is not enough, it is not spiritual enough, and knows too little about the divine realm." We ask them about who God is, saying "Try to answer the question without merely referring to the tenets of Judaism." Jesus constantly nudges His disciples and fellow Jews to the edges of what they know, and then says, in effect, "Keep going." Most Jews will have little tolerance for all of this, and it is best not to waste time with unreceptive people. I frankly don't know that such "conversion" unto Jesus is even possible in Israel on a large scale within, say, twenty years, since their social psychology is so ingrained. Making the Gospels out to be a palatable source of spiritual curiosity could help, such as through YouTube videos. The least familiar option would be to expose traditional Jews to the Shroud of Turin (about which they generally know little), but this requires specialized knowledge, and may not be easily understood.

In regard to what scholars have called replacement theology or supersessionism, Jesus offers no real theology to replace the rituals and practices of Judaism, but by "fulfilling the Law," He transcends its rigid limitations through providing Himself as a direct linkage to God to straddle the chasm between the human and the divine. He is the *who* eclipsing the *what* to gift us Himself as the One who gets baptized in the Jordan River to gain divine status for our benefit. We can tell recalcitrant Jews that He is the path their religion takes to be offered any real sense of what God is all about, that any religion must be subservient to the divine realm, since we did not create ourselves. To use the familiar analogy, Christianity is the snake shedding the skin of limitations Judaism has shackled itself with to be any less dogmatically burdened with the *what* over the *whom*, though it is far from perfect. As I write this, the Methodist church is likely going to splinter over the issue of homosexuality and same-sex marriage, as though any church can actually affect anyone's sexual orientation. Protestants gave up five of the seven Catholic sacraments, but how much better are we for doing so? No religion, by itself, is ever enough, since, in our case, we can "see" the elephant we are all talking about amongst ourselves, yet it remains invisible.

John's Gospel (which, for me, is the greatest of all Scripture) was written late in the 1ˢᵗ Century CE against the backdrop of the first Jewish Christians being banished from synagogues for accepting Jesus Christ as their *Mashiach*. John was the only disciple still alive, but once he was gone, the theological arguments would ensue because there were no more witnesses to Jesus' ministry, and so it has been since then. It was really theology that nearly "replaced" Jesus, not Christianity replacing Judaism. His new covenant melded into the old one as a continuous movement toward God in predicting the loss of the second Temple, and with it the animal sacrifices that would never return. The *whom* had finally replaced the *what* — hence, no third Temple. The schism between Judaism and early Christianity was inevitable for this same reason: there was no Jesus in traditional Judaism, so, for the Christians, it was not enough. The Bible was never enough, and no religion is ever enough. Only Jesus was humanly enough, and only our ever-invisible God is enough. All the books and all the dogmas are left behind should we reach Heaven, and there we shall be blessed with our Lord, who bathes everyone in radiant love — Jews *and* Gentiles — at last.

May 2022

A JEWISH ARGUMENT FOR WHEN JESUS WAS BORN

In at least recent years, Messianic Jews (who also accept *Yeshua* — Jesus their Messiah) have proposed that He was not born during Christmastime, but rather earlier in the year. While their "argument" is not entirely persuasive, it is nonetheless interesting.

The main description of Jesus' birth is found, of course, early in Luke's Gospel. It is important to note that Luke does not specify the time of year when Jesus was born. It is also important to note that late December in Israel can be rather cold (with occasional snow), and so the shepherds would not likely be "tending their flocks by night" outdoors at that time of year. I will come around to the question of why there was "no room for them in the inn" for Joseph and Mary.

Luke's story begins with the pregnancy of Elizabeth with John the Baptist, she being of "barren age." In this "argument," Elizabeth gets pregnant probably in June (possibly during Pentecost or *Shavuot,* which did occur at that time this year, but this is speculative historically), and Mary gets pregnant in December, perhaps on or near December 25th (also speculative, perhaps during *Hanukkah*). Remember, Jews had three major yearly festivals: Passover (*Pesach*), Pentecost and *Sukkot*, or the autumnal Feast of Tabernacles, which celebrated the summer harvest. Hence, John the Baptist was about six months older than Jesus. Luke's business about "the leaping for joy in the womb" may be his own hyperbolic embellishment, yet the point is made.

John the Baptist is then born during springtime's Passover, which could be considered a summation of most or all of the Old Testament prophets, he signaling the coming of their Messiah (*Mashiach*), and so he "gets his own festival." Jesus is then born during the *Sukkot* festival in September or October, roughly six months after John. There is "no room in the inn" because of the large festival crowds in Jerusalem. *Sukkot* is an eight-day festival (this year: October 9-16) when a lot goes on: the erecting of booths (*sukkahs*), or temporary shelters, singing and much merriment, as it is the most celebratory of the three Jewish festivals. Jesus would have been born on the first day of *Sukkot*, and circumcised on the eighth or last day of the festival. Thus, He is born, circumcised and resurrected on Sunday, and since His original followers were largely still Jewish, it could have been them more than the early Christian church who saw Sunday as the proper day for worship of their newly-found *Mashiach.*

Some people think that Christmas grew out of a Roman pagan festival called *Saturnalia*, based upon an earlier Greek festival, which included gift-giving. Pope Julius I decreed the December 25th date for Jesus' birth only in the 4th Century, for somewhat unclear reasons. Christmas has evolved a lot over the centuries, including the Nordic fellow, "Kris Kringle" (a precursor to our Santa Claus) and the use of decorated trees.

If the Jews are right, then God was using their festivals to bring two very important figures into the world within a year's time, in close proximity to the death of the last Jewish king, Herod the Great, in ca. 4 BCE. In John's Gospel, Jesus goes to *Sukkot* one time, where He famously proclaimed that "those who are thirsty, come drink," based on a festival water ritual.

You might ask: Does it really matter when Jesus was born? Well, didn't you want to know when your own children were born?

June 2022

OF THOSE PREFERABLY LOST TO GOD

The word *testimonial* tends to cleave us toward or against such personal spiritual confessions as either too emotionally messy in public presentation or rather a more accurate sense of our spiritual temperature. The better testimonials draw us in to the speakers for nuances gained along their journeys toward God that can resonate with and nudge us forward. Testimonials by nature are not steeped in either theological or doctrinal concerns, but reveal more personal attempts to answer basic questions about the nature of God in our lives or why religion matters to us. Testimonials are the more personal guts of our faith, when we can sometimes say *Yes* or *No* with greater conviction. I enjoy listening to testimonials when they take us to somewhere spiritually clarifying. Several years ago, I began listening to testimonials on YouTube by Jews who found Jesus to be, if not their *Mashiach*, then at least a source of spiritual solace and connection with God. These are testimonials of real revelation, that something spiritually new truly occurs, sometimes despite intense resistance from more traditional family and friends. These Jews realize that religion, merely for its own sake, is not enough. I noticed that rabbis are virtually never consulted in their times of crisis, perhaps expecting nothing much helpful from them beyond the recitation of the familiar. Testimonials can take us somewhere we have never been, or even never considered. Testimonials are given by those whose faith is suddenly brimming, and we then share their excitement. They are sometimes spiritually contagious, and the best ones affirm that God is no waste of our time.

Against this up-raised fervor of sorts is the more commonplace example of *spiritual malaise*. I have discussed atheism in earlier essays, and such malaise is generally not atheism, as atheists can be as fervent in their "religion" as any firm believers. There is a substantial subset of religious people who, if asked, would never deny their sense that God exists, yet would also admit that they can not yet truly find Him for themselves. They may well go to church regularly and read the Bible at least occasionally, but nothing really sticks. Some are spiritually despondent, while others merely accept their *malaise* with a shrug, as though to say *What shall I do?* Of course, there are also those for whom the whole subject of God and religion really doesn't matter at all. There are likely millions and millions of such people all over the world, and even if they believe in God, He remains at best a distant curiosity and thus worthy of little contemplation. God can not be so easily seen, and all of us lose sight of Him more than occasionally, since *God was never human.* It is these people, bothered and unbothered by their *malaise* or their dimmer faith, that I want to discuss, because they are anathema to every church's calling purpose — figuratively or literally sitting in the back pews, wondering why they keep coming, if they do come at all. Before I found a more steadfast faith over the last ten years, there were periods when God was certainly too peripheral for me to consider Him a worthwhile interest, so this is no disinterested discussion for me.

While much has been said and written about the up-lifting aspects of *spiritual awakening*, quite little has been pondered about *spiritual malaise,* particularly our resistance to courting God at all.

*

I will begin with an analogy that doesn't really hold weighable water. If we want to lose weight, for whatever reason, then this comes about from the suddenly obvious sense that we are overweight from either a visual inspection of our bodies or because some kindly person tells us we could "lose a few pounds." If we are successful in losing weight, then the need to do so has become internalized or *introjected* well enough to plan diets, exercise or, in more dire circumstances, have bariatric surgery. Our need to lose weight comes from what we see, translated into what we feel ("worry"), which results in a promising course of action that leads to eventual success. Of course, there is also "falling off the wagon" or "back-sliding," which are also church terms for either sin or "less than righteous behavior." My point is that weight loss results from feel and sight, leveraged into positive action that makes us thinner and thus happier.

My analogy goes hollow once we get to the subject of God — specifically, His invisibility. I discussed this in a previous essay, and so I will only say here that this serves as *the* principal problem for those experiencing *spiritual malaise*, and indeed, all of us, no matter how spiritually inclined we are. How many times in these essays have I remind us that *no one sees God?* Thus, there is no midriff bulge, chronic fatigue or sweating easily in the summer from excess poundage. Not even a kindly person is likely to say to us *You could use a little extra spirituality.* All us of start at something akin to the Western Wall in Jerusalem: a remnant of what matters, though the whole can not be well-enough conjured by anyone. It is not surprising that Jews stopped using animal sacrifices to alleviate their sins once the Second Temple was destroyed by the Romans in 70 CE. The religious milieu of the sacrifices had again been lost, hundreds of years after the first Temple was destroyed by the Babylonians in 586 BCE, and they just did not have the stomach to build a third Temple, because their introjection in the form of a stone sanctuary had twice been ruined. It is simply far too late for a third Temple. So the Jews have lost their Temples, their Ark of the Covenant and their animal sacrifices, but have regained their own country. Are they now as spiritually inclined as in "the old days?" Probably not, yet they still have their festivals and other rituals, though I have called this *religion for religion's sake,* trying to make the invisible visible.

Catholics have their rosary beads and repeatable prayers, and all Christians have both the Apostles' and Nicene Creeds, if we wish. But none of this truly makes the invisible visible, and this problem of *no religion ever being enough,* is the heart of spiritual malaise. What I eventually learned, after decades in and out of church, was that church attendance didn't work either, at least not for me.

Once we say "*I believe in God,*" we are then faced with a certain feeling which I think some people would almost call *dread.* Dread because of "all the unknowables" that come with being involved with God and perhaps some particular religion, say Christianity. These *unknowables* are what make atheism so appealing for some 3-10% of people, because they are materialistically eliminated and life becomes simpler. The atheistic problem is that the rest of us don't believe their naïve, child-like simplicity, since we didn't create ourselves, and the universe is not really random in its Natural workings. So spiritually-inclined people have to try to deal with the following list of the *unknowables*, either with intention or, more often, letting them slide to the sides of our faith:

- The likelihood that, even if we reach Heaven, we will never directly experience either the look or sound of God, at least how we would do so on Earth. He thus still remains an eternal mystery, even in His "absent appearance."

- For some or many people, this really matters: how do we know if we are going to Heaven, and what are God's "criteria" to get there?

- For me, I have come to understand why God allows evil in the world. A much harder question is why does He allow such horrendous destruction from hurricanes, since they evolve from weather and not from our sins?

- We know that God answers some prayers, most often in hospitals in times of medical crisis, but again, what are His "criteria?"

- Since God must have existed before the universe began, and He waited for billions of years before human beings came into the world on at least one planet, how does He maintain His eternal patience for all of our endless screw-ups? Even Jesus, far more human than God, would sometimes become exasperated with us.

- What is it really like to have "a personal relationship with God" that is different from a traditional human relationship? How do we know when it is "in effect" and is it more fleeting than steadfast until we reach Heaven?

- What did Jesus say and do while here on earth, aside from what the Gospels tell us about Him? What actually happened must have been different than how He is portrayed in these four vignettes? Only John's Gospel sometimes approximates eyewitnessing.

There are surely more *unknowables*, but these make the point. If religions tend to provide false certainties to smooth out the knotty questions about God that keep us up at night, then why would many people simply say: *I believe in God, but don't want to think about Him too hard.* These include church-goers, and many more for whom church never much matters. Yes, for Christians there is Jesus, but He lived long ago, and I don't pray to Him anyway. He too is part of the *unknowables*, since none of us has ever met Him, and perhaps never will. Remember, this essay is about *spiritual malaise*, and not frothy evangelism. It is about *we don't care about God, and that is our preference.* I too was almost there once. It is not atheism — it is actually worse.

*

Taking more than a slight detour, I want to talk about money, particularly how it can reflect our spirituality. Paul famously intoned *"the love of money* is the root of all evil," which is not true. Evil is the root of itself, as often money is not involved in either torture, rape or murder. How much does money preoccupy us beyond paying our bills and saving for our future is what interests me here. Money as a preoccupation in itself beyond financial survival or even comfort. Hoarding our wealth for its own sake, as the selfishly rich tend to do. Buying extravagances that are otherwise unnecessary for our well-being, such as expensive cars, boats or houses. Wealth as an expression of our spiritual malaise. What was Charles Dickens getting at with his famous character of Ebeneezer Scrooge? Scrooge, of course, suffered from spiritual malaise until, God, in the form of the three ghosts, wizened him up just in time for Christmas Day.

Money as the self-expression of our personal preferences against more charitable gifts of money and time in the service of others. This is not some religious false dichotomy, akin to faith versus works, physical versus spiritual or science versus religion. Even the most charitable person will still buy personal items, sometimes of serious expense. But what is the thrust of how we spend our available "free money," and whom does it benefit? How easily do we part with charitable money? How closely do we watch our assets, such as in the stock market, and how pained do we feel when we lose a significant amount of money in a day? We all want a comfortable retirement, but what financial form does this take with our spendable money? Do our charitable contributions increase as a function of greater wealth? For those of us not used to ten percent of our income being tithed to a church, we then must decide ourselves how charitable to be. Even tithing does not necessarily ease our *spiritual malaise*, since it can readily be construed as a "church duty."

What am I saying about money? That the influence of God is present or absent in how we spend our available money in a manner acceptable to ourselves as psychological and spiritually necessary. Where does the bulk of our "free money" go and for whose benefit? A slight cure for spiritual malaise is to give away at least a little more money on occasions than we can easily part with, and see how discomforting this feels — a bit like Scrooge giving Bob Cratchit Christmas Eve off from work. Jesus asked too much of the Heaven-seeking rich man, while He and the disciples were financially supported by the kindly benevolence of several women. I never gave any serious amount of money to charities when I was younger, not because I was so selfish, but because the need to do so was not yet spiritually necessary, though I am admittedly still too charitably slack.

*

So what is *spiritual malaise*? Let me first say what it is *not*. It is not psychological depression or political disinterest or cultural complacency in the face of nagging social or environmental problems. It is not solely a modern concern, but has been around since religions began. Most importantly, it does not go away on its own, and so can last for decades. *Spiritual malaise* is our personal inability to "sight" God, to feel Him inside us — not for a day or week, but for months or years. It is an estrangement which becomes duller with time, when God can get "forgotten." He stops being of real personal interest, stops hovering even at the periphery of our lives, and so is written off as unreachable. He almost ceases to exist, for us. It is "the dark night of the soul." In my solar system analogy, we have strangely moved from one of the inner planets around the sun out to where the light takes so long to reach us it is always cold. It is the spiritual outer planets.

What is awful is that neither God nor us has seemingly done anything for this to happen. We have simply lost sight of who God is and why He matters, and too many of us don't care. For too many of us, *spiritual malaise* is a natural consequence of either no church or poorly-inspiring church as children, and so, from a young age, God is cast off to the outer reaches of our galaxy, and perhaps never returns. I first left church as a teen-ager, and could not "sight" God again for nearly 15 years to any serious degree. I was not an atheist — I just couldn't find Him. I have since come to understand that, for myself at least, God has to be "courted" rather than ignored for us to "sight" Him. I am reminded that Lee Stroebel started out as an atheist before becoming a pastor as described in his book and film, *The Case For Christ* (1998). He fought off God until he had to surrender, because nothing else made sense to him. As I have said before, *God has an ego*.

I have talked about how our narcissism affects our faith in God at various points in both my book and in these essays. How do we "make room" for God in both our spiritual consciousness as well as in our daily lives? Without such "making room," there is no spirituality, but how does that happen? While in many cases, it is sparked by meeting a spiritual person(s), in my own case it was first provoked by learning about the Shroud of Turin forty years ago. Occasionally, Jews meet Christians who "turn them on" to Jesus. But more often, such spiritual people are turned down by those with *spiritual malaise* because they "just don't have time for God." The many spiritual questions easily bog us down with their "what ifs" and our inability to actually see He who forms the figure of our devotion. This is why Jesus was and is so important, because He could be seen and heard, and that would have proven to be invaluable to the Jews longing for their Lord. God tells us that Jesus was His evolving man-god on Earth sent to us in human form to be spiritually persuasive that Yahweh exists and loves us. *Spiritual malaise* knows this, but finds it dusty and too irrelevant to daily life, since there are so many other matters to deal with and live through. *Spiritual malaise* says "I believe in God, but have neither the time nor the interest to either ponder or emulate Him." There is no real effort to "make room for God." I knew this as a daily reality for years and years until, ten years ago, something clicked, and I began to "make a lot of room" for God on a daily basis. There are many ways to "make room for God," but without doing so, there is no true spirituality taking place. Reading the Gospels (particularly Mark and John) is a good start, but merely attending church, no matter how regularly, is not enough. I knew that, too.

In this essay's title, I speak of *spiritual malaise* as a *preference*, but how so? Not really by choice, but by settling into a preference over years and decades because there is no serious desire to do anything else in trying to better find God. For too many people — even church-goers — God proves to be an insurmountable impediment to Himself — too vague and too invisible too much of the time. The Bible does not really answer either my questions listed above nor others asked by each of us. It is easier to settle more comfortably into Christian history and church practices than to try to answer any of these or other questions. It is easier to not try, and it is easier to give up asking. For me, something clicked and I had to start asking, to finally become *spiritually curious*, which is the best remedy for *spiritual malaise*. How did I do so? Most simply, I left church and took on the job of learning, thinking and writing for myself. I don't know any other way. It has been a long but rewarding journey, and so I do not regret it, because *I had to do something else*. God finally matters enough to me, rather later in life — but as I say, *Better later than even later.*

November 2022

160

SUMMING UP: TWO (PROSE) POEMS

LISTEN TO ALL THAT IS LORDLY TELLABLE

What you would call My hands fashioned everything you see & taste that stays unconjured by your human doings,despite all of your techno-progress you only hear because I allow silence & the music it ravishes to tickle your ear-drums for the overwhelming surety that *only I ever-lastingly matter.* You keep speculating that there was necessarily some thin yesterday when I never existed,tho your own aging rattles your sense of My impalpable immortality,tiny & huge as I am as the Natural majesty unfindable amidst your micro-chips,let Me be Myself & you might survive. There was no life & there was only slowly-evolving life, there was always light & air & water along with this tectonic crunching of the ground to up-raise the land to hills & mountains before anything crawled or flew air-borne,I made & watched it all as the finest scientist to never own any prize,so I laugh when you think your discoveries brighten your horizons farther than I already possess. In your laboratories or at your conferences,no one asks *who is this daedal being who always eclipsed the wealth of our knowledge,who without instruments or computers calculated the perfection of all living history?*

Cells swelling past the plants & fish,past the insects & the other mammals toward you who uprightly rose to seek Me skyward as the first ones asking *are we the final surprise of life,* cultures & the gods of your making to explain how I work,silly soap opera gods & goddesses scheming & fighting in the sky expressing the whims of your imagination — this foolery what the Israelites inherited to shrink such godly mayhem down to one Creator,worshipped & forgotten in ardor or idolatry until I wearied of how you only wrongly reject Me,since I never wrote anything but truly gifted you the workable mercy of life as it squirms & shouts. I was never some bunch of old stories recitable by children in the summertime while singing & playing in rusted churches lost to who I purely am. To memorize & study the Bible is to glimpse what you could say about Me, tho I am no quotable living Scripture,but My hands & My benevolence are silently befitting you with your nimbler sense of My grace,   mystery filling the vacuum between you & I that I will never describe to you,because you will smelt it into something crudely teachable,tho what you suck from Me aligns you rightly.

I gave thumbs & thinking about yourselves to have you look for Me in sky & soul beyond all other creatures Ark-borne before & after tragedy's grinning signatures,I knew you were always the unshrunken gluttony of feasting upon idols carved & sensuous,to fondle & drool as clutchable signs of Me to be buried in graves,as later came the Crosses for the votively righteous—-such nothing between you & I not plastic but edible,lending lyrics to songs about "forgettable Me" to receive all that is earthly cherishable then & now,since psyche gobbles religion & spits out its doctrinal carcasses. I became exhausted by the arguments & the clerical pedigrees,the selfishness of those who falsely understood Me against those still heralding My favour---all of you beguiled by your own stupid rumours that I could somehow be theologized in sermons & wafers as *our God we know*,how I love you known to no one else besides My wonder-full Son.

Jesus is admittedly no one without Me,I breathed Myself into Him at His birth & gemmed His spine with everything you could witness & ponder,I told Him to startle you awake to shed your deader religion to recover Me beyond stories & Scripture as your radiating Creator—no Trinitarian system inexplicable in its circular gaseous confusion,but rather how I flooded Him with My sense of your worldly purpose—Jesus sometimes still smiles at Me,tho He wonders about the wilting realm of His crucifixional gift, *the weight of our wisdom being what uglier tonnage.*

June 2017

HEAVEN-LESS WEDNESDAY

I was born of a girl well-fathered
by God's blessing to be divinely raised
      in human dominion
to wizen the world from the rising time
of my Jewish puberty on thru to
My long apprenticeship in both carpentry
& studying the Law before My mission
was baptized by my gruffer cousin,
I wandered in Galilee for several years
teaching our people about the unseen
      Kingdom of our mercy-full Lord,
healing the afflicted & rebuking Pharisees
for your hard hearts & shackled vision,
beguiled by learned power & cynical trespass
against God's desire for all to be loved—-
all has gone on,for & against Me,
I accepted & rejected as a holier salesman
of a cause called *righteous salvation*,
tasted by many but swallowed & choked out.

I have come to Jerusalem more than once,
walking the dry,thirsty distance from Nazareth
or elsewhere for one of our yearly festivals
as is our custom,
      Jerusalem's temple
of sacrifices & skekel-debt,of mouthings
& corruption while suffering under the Romans,
God brought Me into this crueler time
of zealotry & crucifixion to ease hatred
by abrading the terrorable with the divine—-
      again it is Passover,
when our people swell in faith & purpose
in our travels to arrive at our shrine
& our sanctuary,where God bequeaths us.

Come & follow Me I commanded you,
        My twelve brethren
of our tribal history melded to My work
for you to spread Me in our diaspora
after My death,
                wiser than many
too smart to know where God shows Himself
to any of us seeable thru our flesh
to witness everything impalpably His—-
        I leave you confused
from each instance of my reckoning
& thru talking amongst yourselves
ask Me the same questions everyone else
ponders: *Are You the man-god-bridge
between our Lord & us,looking behind You
shall we find Him?*
                You are the bread
I offer to those who can not eat of Me
on their own,you are My face for those
of this world in My sending you to them,
        I sense your weariness
doing this work of sprouting God in people
s' hearts,being the seeds of your coming
betrayal of Me—-
                you will save Me
for years until they kill all of you sooner
than grievances can be murderously eased,
such is the sad gamble our Lord made
with Himself to create us for His amusement.

I took three of you to the mountaintop
to show you our Father's divine faith
in Me, I glowed whiter than our Law
's congested pretense that words are men
who willingly forego ourselves to love
even our enemies,
                radiant as I must be
to lead you thru the desert of your doubts
about Me this late in our pearlish journey,
I riving one from another thru uttered truth.

I healed a blind man before the Pharisees,
who disbelieved what your own eyes saw
to accuse his parents of eye-fully lying,
since God gifted us no swallowable doctrines
with which to sever ourselves from Him
to berate & blaspheme. I resurrected Lazurus
on the fourth day after he died
to prove God never accepts our customs,
that resurrection comes according to His Will
& not to please how many manly abstractions
stuffed into books? I over-turned
the money-changers' tables yesterday
outside the Temple to relieve the poor
of the oppressive shekel tax,a fresh
-ly incendiary act of what men could do
in the name of He who up-raises us,
how we cannibalize our Jewish future.

                    *

It is during what someone will later
call Passion Week,after a donkey ride
foretold by Zechariah & again preaching
in our Temple,crumbling it if I wished
to tell you I will be your working church,

that God calls Me to out-stretch all
you could conjure as to His majesty
past votive slogans & slaughtered lambs,
I sit here today & tonight praying aloud
in the Mount of Olives,twitchier over
what is yawning,blood & sleep riled
amongst we leaders. No one ever says
to Me *You have failed to be persuasive,*

tho the doubt-full daily nibble upon Me
one after another,since *no one sees God*
to crown Me with any truthy halo---
            I am more than merely human

yet what I say & do gets stopped
by your selfish senses,
                       smally devilish
given I have shown all that is possible

by anyone other than our gracious Lord
Himself,confirming Me.
                       Tomorrow
of our own Jewish vipers,convince-able
by no measure of all I know more than
any of you,
                       a lamb only licking faces
& not strung from a nailish tree
to flex its worthiness to man & God,

I tremble in the looming sufferage
that martyrs brand our predicaments
upon the souls of those who love us,
while everyone else wonders why evil
claims a thousand names,imminently forever.

March 2018